We Know What to Do

Also by Lamar Alexander

FRIENDS: JAPANESE AND TENNESSEANS
(with Robin Hood)
STEPS ALONG THE WAY
SIX MONTHS OFF
THE NEW PROMISE OF AMERICAN LIFE
(co-edited with Chester E. Finn, Jr.)

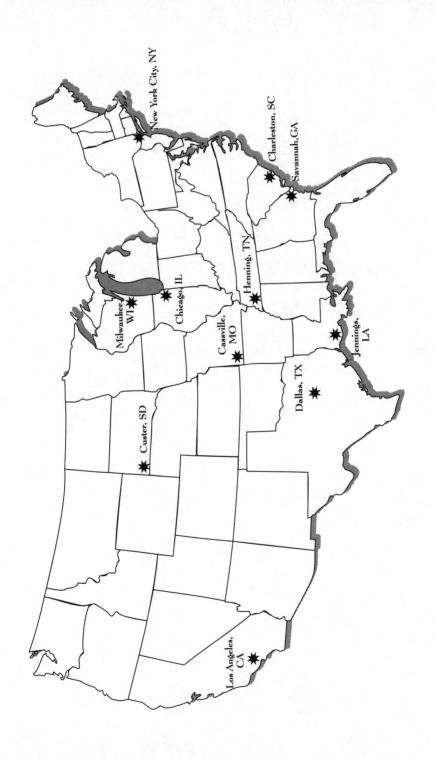

We Know What to Do

A Political Maverick Talks with America

LAMAR ALEXANDER

WILLIAM MORROW AND COMPANY, INC.
New York

It is the policy of William Morrow and Company, Inc., and its imprints and affiliates, recognizing the importance of preserving what has been written, to print the books we publish on acid-free paper, and we exert our best efforts to that end.

Library of Congress Cataloging-in-Publication Data

Alexander, Lamar.
    We know what to do : a political maverick talks with America / by Lamar Alexander.
        p.   cm.
    ISBN 0-688-14288-5 (hc)
        1. United States—Politics and government—1993–
    2. Presidents—United States—Election—1996.   I. Title.
    E885.A44   1995
    324.973'0929—dc20   95-21711
                                                                          CIP

Printed in the United States of America

First Edition

1   2   3   4   5   6   7   8   9   10

BOOK DESIGN BY PAUL CHEVANNES

To Honey, Drew, Leslee, Kathryn, and Will, who have gone where I went and seen what I saw—not all the time, but during the best parts.

*

My parents and my hometown, Maryville, Tennessee, gave me "everything I needed that was important" so that I could understand and enjoy the promise of American life.

My share of the profits from this book will go to Maryville High School for college scholarships for outstanding graduates, to Maryville College for a music scholarship in my parents' honor, and to the Boy Scout and Explorer activities of Troop 88 at the New Providence Presbyterian Church in Maryville.

LAMAR ALEXANDER
PHOTOGRAPH BY EARL WARREN

Foreword
On the Road Again

On a Sunday afternoon our daughter Kathryn, a soph-
omore in college, called home as I was leaving the
house to make a speech. She asked, "About what?"

"About the American Dream," I said.

"Dad, a lot of my friends don't believe there is an
American Dream anymore."

In a year when doubt and division were rampant in
America, I decided to drive across the country to
make sure I understood why my daughter's friends
felt this way.

I was in the process of making up my mind about
running for president in 1996, but this was not a campaign swing. I have found in public life that it is very

easy to slip out of touch, but easy enough to get back. So I set out to do what a lot of Americans do: drive across the country between July Fourth and Labor Day. What was different about this trip was that I spent the night mostly with people I had never met before, had supper with them, and stayed up late talking.

We were usually a traveling squad of four or five. Lewis Lavine organized the trip. Scott Hamilton, a former staffer at the Department of Education, made most of the stops. Earl Warren and John Danielson rotated along the way, working out the logistics. My son Drew and his friend Rob Gluck helped with the driving.

At Bubba's Barbecue in Eureka Springs, Arkansas, not so far from Branson, Missouri, a curious white-haired lady watched closely as four of us settled into our seats. "Well," she asked, "which quartet are you?" Perhaps it was our casual, rumpled dress that made her mistake us for gospel musicians.

In the eight weeks I cruised along the roadways, I had ample time to think, to reflect, to talk to myself (and into a tape recorder). The stories and lessons of that drive, which are at the heart of the book, are from Americans who are living their lives in ways that suggest to the rest of us what we need to do. Their answers might not work everywhere, for everyone. Nor are there answers here for all the questions we need to ask. But in the everyday lives of these men and women, we found abundant evidence of the confidence and resilience that make this such a remarkable country.

I had a map *and* a point I hoped to prove: that these answers we are urgently seeking are already known to us. We know how to live with each other, how to raise our children, how to make our streets safer, our schools better, and how to remind ourselves of what is most important. We know what to do, but many of us are not doing it. The answer stares us in the face, and for the most part, we just stare back—or into our television sets.

The nation is clearly off track. We can feel that in our everyday lives. But it is not for the usual reasons.

Here we are at peace in the world. The economy is growing. There is one superpower and we're it. Twenty-five percent of the world's money is in our pockets (with just 4 percent of the world's population). We win most of the Nobel Prizes. Our universities are the ones everyone wants to attend. At any given moment, people are packed into small boats, clinging to rafts, swimming and wading and running to reach our borders, desperate to live in this country. Yet we are grumpy.

No one remembers when we were so out of sorts. We felt better when we were at war. Then, at least, we knew what we were about, who we were, and what was most important to us. We are far enough into something we call the Telecommunications Age now that we know and feel it, and it has turned our lives upside down. Today the pollsters say Americans by a margin of two to one believe our country is badly off track.

And among parents, two thirds believe their children

will not have as good a quality of life as they have had—the first generation of parents in our history to think that.

We are, it can be argued, just going through what everybody else is going through. We have changed eras. All the balls are in the air. No one has a fix on what comes next. Look how worried Europe is. The republics of the former Soviet Union are struggling with democracy. East Germany is giving all of Germany indigestion. Japan's prime ministers turn over faster than Italy's once did. So everyone is in trouble. Back to TV.

Not so fast. This restiveness, this off-trackness, this lack of confidence, this lack of hope, is bigger trouble for us than for any other country. To begin with, we are still the lead horse. If we don't know where we are headed, it is harder for everyone else to know.

But more important, when we lose faith that our tomorrow will be better than today, we lose what makes us special. It would be as if England had lost its past, or France its capacity to be civilized, or China its patience. In *The Promise of American Life,* Herbert Croly wrote in 1909 that the promise "is the unlimited belief in the future of America. The faith of Americans in their own country is religious, if not in its intensity, at any rate in its absolute and universal authority. It pervades the air we breathe. As children we hear it asserted or implied in the conversation of our elders. . . . The skeptic is not controverted; he is overlooked."

Nearly a century after Croly wrote his book we seem

to be losing America's special claim on greatness, our confidence in our unlimited future, and the principle that this future is available to anyone who will make an effort. We are losing it even though we know exactly what to do about it. I believe we are in much more trouble today than we have any reason to be.

That was why on July 4, 1994, the day after my fifty-fourth birthday, I set out from my home in Nashville, Tennessee, to drive for eight weeks and 8,800 miles across America. I wanted to remind myself of what we need to do. So I went to where the answers are.

Out there on the interstates and back roads of America, even the roads themselves remind you what a magnificent country this is. When our family lived for six months in Australia a few years ago, one Aussie said to me, "Do you realize that no other country has an interstate system like you Americans have?" I had never thought of that. And this mobility is as good a symbol as we have of our freedom and the promise of America. Anybody can get on the interstate and go anywhere they want, do what they want, as far as they want, for as long as they want.

The whole story of America is on those roads, the signs of greatness and the signs of troubles. You can even do a little light reading as you go. A bumper sticker on Interstate 10 in Louisiana said, MAKE WELFARE AS HARD TO GET AS A BUILDING PERMIT. Another one in South Carolina said, I LOVE MY COUNTRY, BUT I FEAR MY GOVERNMENT.

Where I roamed, there is very little interest in reinventing America, and in particular letting it be done from Washington, D.C. There is a great deal of interest in reminding ourselves what made this such a great country in the first place.

A Cherokee woman in eastern Oklahoma said, "We are not taking the time to think about what is most important to us and to pass it down. We don't take the time to remember what we need to hold fast and true."

Nearly everyone I met believes that the answers are in our homes, shops, diners, meeting halls, community centers, and in the classrooms, synagogues, and churches. It doesn't take long to be reminded of how important religious beliefs are in the lives of most of us—not as a political movement but in the deep faith of many kinds expressed in everyday activities.

Let me be more specific about what I heard at the supper table and in my late-evening conversations. But let me start with what I didn't hear. All summer the Washington newspapers were consumed by Whitewater and health-care reform. In two months I probably heard less than half an hour of opinion, total, on those subjects. And those few minutes were devoted to health care.

What I heard about was crime. People are afraid to take walks in their neighborhoods, and not just in the big cities.

Everyone has a welfare story. In Cassville, Missouri, I visited with a couple who knew exactly what the federal benefits were in their area. They wonder why some of their friends can make more money by not working than they do working.

In Dallas, at a homeless shelter, or in Pensacola, where the military is cutting back, there is fretful talk about jobs and the future. Even though the economy is growing, every year 10 percent of working Americans still lose their jobs. Those who do almost always find new ones, but it is hard to count on anything when conditions are so turbulent.

Talk of jobs usually leads to talk about education. Parents worry about losing control of their schools to the bureaucrats, to the social engineers, and to Hollywood values. They worry about the safety of their children, and whether they are learning enough to survive in the new job market.

If anything struck me during my eight weeks on the road, it was the intensity of the feelings about the national government, a sense of outrage and exasperation with its size, spending, meddling, and arrogance.

I can count on one hand the number of people who said that the crime bill passed in 1994 would make their streets safer. In Baton Rouge, the sheriff said he didn't want it and probably won't hire any of the 100,000 new police officers because "in two years the money will be gone and I'll have the employees and no way to pay them."

The government in Washington devours our paycheck, promises too much, delivers too little, pretends to do things we know very well it can't, tells people to do things they don't want to do, and then insists we pay the bill. You can understand why Washington has come to be regarded as a company town that has grown too big for its britches. What my friends in Washington are missing is that this time it's different. It is the whole town: the Congress, the president, the bureaucrats, the media, the talk shows, the think tanks. They all seem to be sitting up there telling us that we are too stupid or too uncaring to decide for ourselves what to do about the things that worry us the most. The sense of outrage among mainstream Americans should not be underestimated.

The longer I drove, the more stops I made, the more clearly I could see the change coming that produced the Republican Congress in Washington. I saw the anger at the arrogance of Washington that caused this shift of power. But I also noticed a greater concern was in the hearts and on the lips of almost everyone I met. Now that I have completed this book, I feel this worry running through almost every page. It is the same concern I believe you would find if you were to walk outside your house and ask the first ten people you see what they believe is the greatest problem facing our country, the number-one reason we seem to be losing our confidence in our future. I believe most would say it is the breakdown of the family. No particular political group has a monopoly on this concern. It is everyone's concern. Our ability to recapture the promise of American life depends on the strength of the family, the neighborhood, the churches and synagogues, and the schools of this country. These are the most important things.

Halfway through the drive, I found a good way to take the country's pulse—by asking those I visited this question: Looking ahead twenty years, do you believe your children and grandchildren will have more opportunities living in this country than you have had? Most people were afraid to say yes.

My own answer to the question is absolutely yes, because I am going to do everything within my power to see that my children and grandchildren have those opportunities. On my drive I found plenty of other people who feel the same way, people who know exactly what to do and are doing it—people leading everyday lives with an extraordinary belief in what makes America special. This is a book of their stories.

Contents

We Know What to Do

FRED MONTGOMERY

PHOTOGRAPH BY EARL WARREN

CHAPTER 1

The Most Important Things

HENNING, Tennessee

Our neighborhood in Nashville is where this drive across America actually began. It is a neighborhood of families and wide streets and sidewalks and old city houses. It is also the location of the annual Whitland Avenue Fourth of July Celebration and Parade—the finest old-fashioned red, white, and blue Fourth of July picnic held anywhere in the U.S.A.

On Saturday, the second of July, 1994, flags had begun to appear along Whitland Avenue. The Burtons' house had the most, by some estimates twenty different American and state flags. Their front yard would be where the symphony would sit and the podium would go. By Sunday there was a small flag at the curb-

1

side of every house on Whitland and on most of the cross streets, including ours. Pat Burton was solemnly supervising the unloading of the Portalets. Slick Lawson, who had begun planning this year's parade the day after last year's was over, displayed the official sign in his front yard that said that on the next day, July 4, Whitland Avenue would be closed. Juli and Ralph Mosely had worked all day on the corn casserole, their contribution to the covered dish picnic.

The newspaper on the morning of the Fourth said it would soon be 97 degrees. Already the temperature was racing in that direction. The air was sticky, but the clouds were too high to be threatening. By 10:00 A.M. all the parking places on Whitland were filled. Cars that we had never seen before began to line up on our street, too. By eleven the streets were filled with people.

The celebration began at noon when Rabbi Kantor read a letter written in 1790 from the Hebrew Congregation in Savannah, Georgia, to George Washington. A retired brigadier general who flew sixty missions in the Second World War led the Pledge of Allegiance. Sixty volunteers from the Nashville Symphony performed Copeland's "Lincoln Portrait." Henry Arnold delivered the Declaration of Independence with such enthusiasm that grown men shouted "Yes!" I made "The Speech," keeping it brief, talking about how my late friend Alex Haley used to say his favorite six words, "Find the Good and Praise It," especially to people who were busy finding everything wrong with America. It was a strong message coming from the grandson of slaves, from the

2

man who wrote *Roots* and *The Autobiography of Malcolm X.* The symphony played the 1812 Overture. Mothers covered children's ears in preparation for a cannon's twenty-one salutes. The parade commenced, and hungry neighbors began unpacking covered dishes. If King George had been anywhere in the vicinity, he would have gotten away quickly.

The parade featured sweating headbands, tank tops and jeans, motorcycles with riders in gorilla suits, red, white, and blue festooned tricycles, and friends hugging friends who hadn't seen each other since the last Fourth of July. Singer Marshall Chapman slipped up and said, "If you run for president, why don't you use 'Alexander's Ragtime Band'?"

＊

As the parade wound down, I walked home to finish packing the Ford Explorer and to change into more comfortable clothes for the road. Honey, my wife, quietly observed my preparations and then said, "May I ask about the wing-tipped shoes? They don't go with khakis and a polo shirt."

She was right, of course, as she usually is. I had forgotten to change my shoes. "Well, I know what I'd like to wear," I said, and I raced back upstairs to my closet and grabbed my favorite boots, the ones I had worn when I walked across Tennessee in 1978.

I pulled them on. They looked scruffy—but felt good. Honey nodded. "Better than the wing-tips," she said.

The boots had earned their scruffiness. I had put a

thousand miles on those boots, walking for six months across the state, through factories and down main streets and into the homes of people I hoped to serve as governor. I had even returned them to L. L. Bean to see if they could be rejuvenated, but Bean had sent them back. "Beyond repair," they had said. So feeling just as secure and as comfortable as I had on that earlier journey, I kissed Honey good-bye and headed out the door for a drive that would take me eighty-eight thousand miles through thirty-seven states and would last until Labor Day. I would be staying most nights in private homes, mostly with people I had never met before. Just as I had on my walk across Tennessee, I wanted to stay up late talking with them and their friends, learning as much as I could about their lives and the mood of our country.

"The only thing that looks worse than wing-tips with khakis," Honey called out with a final warning, "are wing-tips with white socks!"

We pulled onto Interstate 40 at about 2:00 P.M. The driving was easy. It does not take long, driving out of Nashville, to be out in the countryside. The corn in the fields was coming on well, some of it high enough to cover the bottom of billboards. The Interstate medians were filled with Queen Anne's lace, black-eyed Susans, and daisies—an improvement, I thought, over keeping the grass cut so neatly that wildflowers couldn't grow. The kudzu was in full growth. It had been so wet it seemed as if the plants were straining to let the sun draw out the water. It was too early in the summer for everything to be brown and dry.

Our Ford Explorer is fire-engine red. You can see it coming for a couple of miles. I sat high behind the wheel, but not quite high enough to see over the new center-lane rail guards that block the view of the houseboats on the Tennessee River.

We had been on the road for two hours when we passed the Casey Jones home and railroad museum at exit 87, outside Jackson. I drove off and stopped at a Texaco station, bought a Dr Pepper, filled it with salted peanuts, and drank it, just the way I did when I was a boy. It didn't make any sense. I just wanted to do it.

It was 5:00 P.M. when we drove into Henning. This town of twelve hundred hasn't made the AAA TripTik yet, but it is a dot on the Rand McNally map. The sign at the city limits said HOME OF ALEX HALEY and the bank sign said 98 degrees.

I found Fred Montgomery, the mayor, who would be my host for the evening, in the city hall where several local officials and a few others had assembled. When I arrived, they were talking about Henning's first drive-by shooting. Someone had pumped buckshot into the middle-school principal's front door. Not one person thought the federal crime bill the Congress was then debating in Washington would make any difference. No one suggested calling the governor. They thought they knew where the responsibility lay, and they were discussing what *they* should do. Idea number one was

5

a 9:00 P.M. curfew for their children. Idea number two was a community code of parental responsibility that they would ask every parent to sign.

"How about a city ordinance that makes every parent responsible when their child tears up someone else's property?" was idea number three. "I agree with that," said someone else. "If every parent was fined a thousand dollars every time a child did anything like that, it would put a stop to it. I don't know a better way to shore anybody up than to hit their billfold."

The late afternoon assemblage then proceeded to dispense enough wisdom, if it had all been accepted, to put the country back on track by suppertime. Beginning with this: "There are too many working parents trying to make a living and nobody's raising the kids." Then this: "If the kids can't depend on Mom and Dad, they're going to find somebody else they can depend on. That's why they turn to gangs. We've had gangs for forty years. It's nothing new. If the kids were as afraid of their parents as they are of the gangs, they would stop joining the gangs. We had better be careful: When your town goes down to the ground you can't get it back."

A lady chimed in: "Lack of discipline is the biggest problem in the schools." Someone said: "If I got a whipping in school I got one at home." Someone else: "We got in trouble when we lost prayer in the schools."

Bill Nelson, the police chief, spoke up: "Out of about twelve hundred people who live in this town, ten at most cause almost all the trouble. They would steal anything that wasn't tied down. Some would steal your car with you in it. They mainly deal in drugs, and get connected with the bad elements from the city."

A man interrupted the chief: "The kids aren't getting the benefits of the gimme programs. Sixty percent of the people who get food stamps don't use them for food. They sell them for fifty cents on the dollar."

"That's the problem with federal programs," explained a city councilman. "We could do better if we could make more decisions. Washington doesn't know what Henning needs."

I asked a county commissioner up for reelection what the issues were. He replied: "They are saying to me, 'Mr. Burns, this year we want to clean out the courthouse and get all new people. We need to get back to the basics.' People care about the deficit, crime, leadership, and welfare reform."

∗

Mayor Montgomery had been catching crappie for several days and freezing them, and his family was busy at the school gymnasium frying the fish, frying potatoes, frying hush puppies, mixing big bowls of salad, and filling large glasses with ice for tea. We abandoned our discussion and hurried to the gym. Fred said the blessing and we plunged into the food.

By the time we had finished eating and visiting, it was near dark. The sound of firecrackers exploded from every direction. "Do we have time to go by Alex's house?" I asked the mayor, knowing full well that

would please him as much as it would please me. Fred
Montgomery was Alex Haley's best boyhood friend.

So we drove a few blocks to what had been the home
of Will Palmer, now the Alex Haley Museum. Will Palmer was Alex's grandfather. It was at this home in the
summer evenings that Alex would sit on front porch
steps and listen while his grandma and great-aunt Liz
rocked on the porch and told the stories of Kunta Kinte
and their African ancestors that later became the story
of *Roots*. Alex used to say with a twinkle in his eye that
his grandma, rocking on that porch, telling those stories, could knock a lightning bug out of the air at fourteen feet with an accurate stream of tobacco juice!

Fred led us from room to room, pausing to explain
the faded photographs on the walls. He took us to another time.

They had grown up in houses three blocks apart,
with an old buckboard path between them. They met
when Alex was three, Fred a year older. Alex was in his
yard, tossing a ball. Fred was walking by. In the way of
little boys, neither said a word. "We just looked at each
other and started playing catch." After that, Fred would
steal a few minutes to play by taking a shortcut to town.
His mother would tell him to put his cap on backward,
which meant, he explained: "I'm looking at your back.
No fooling around."

The boys would play at top speed, Fred explained,
because "I was not supposed to be gone long, and when
Mama said something, you obeyed. Alex met me in the
yard and we'd wrestle two rounds and I'd go home.

Mama never missed me. You didn't question Mama but one time. She'd put you in the dust, knock you down with her broom. She would not let your mind get contaminated. It worked, too."

The kitchen had been restored to the way it was when Alex would sit on the windowsill questioning his grandma about her stories while she cooked biscuits on a wood-burning stove. Not until 1947 had anyone in the Haley family seen anything but hand-churned butter.

The first icebox Fred had ever seen was in the kitchen of the house where Alex was born. "Everybody ate at the table in the kitchen," said Fred. "No one came in after the bell rang and got his or her plate and went elsewhere. No one ate without saying grace. Sometimes in my house it would just be a cup of milk and some cornbread scrambled in it, but you bowed your head. And after grace, everyone at the table said something in reverence to God. We learned to say thank you when we didn't have enough. This was the atmosphere we grew up under."

From every wall, the photographs called out to me: Here was Alex's great-grandma Irene, born a slave. She is buried on these grounds. There is Chicken George, who wrote back to his relatives in Virginia that the soil was so rich in Tennessee "you could cut a pig's tail off and stick it into the ground and within three days a piglet would sprout"; and Queen, the daughter of a slave and an Irish plantation owner, whose life had just been made into a TV miniseries.

There was Tom. The hooded men came for him one night. They ordered him out of the cabin, and tied him to a tree. They stripped his clothes to his waist and then whipped him until he fainted. They stopped because they thought he was dead.

Fred said, "Tom had two daughters, Sis and Liz. Aunt Liz was my first schoolteacher. The toughest and strictest teacher you could ever imagine. The school was up on the hill about two blocks. She walked up there. One big room. One switch as tall as the door. And every morning, she left there walking. She'd stop by the fencerow and break off another switch to replace the one she wore out yesterday.

"It was strange. We never hated her, even though I think she didn't know when to quit whipping. We studied and trained because we were told so often she was the person that had the ability to lead us from ignorance and poverty. The first whipping I got from Aunt Liz—my big sister beat me again when I got home. I knew I was going to get another from my mama. But mama put her hands on the sides of my head and said, 'She done it for your own good, boy. I sent you out there to listen to that teacher and get you learning in your head so you can grow up and get a job to put clothes on your back and food on your table. And the money you have left in your pocket wouldn't be money you have to steal and kill to get.'

"Those values never left me. Going to school wasn't enough. Being the best in the class was only enough. Three things that were like a live mist in every black

10

home. One was prayer. The other was learning, what we call education now. The third was freedom."

*

It had gotten dark. We drove to Fred's frame house. He had invited a few friends over—two teachers, the police chief, who lived next door, a neighbor—and we sat around his living room talking with Ernestine, his wife of fifty-two years.

"You know, Fred," I said, "the atmosphere that you grew up with was not so different from the atmosphere I grew up with. I remember when I was appointed education secretary, one newspaper said, 'Lamar Alexander grew up in a lower-middle-class family in a small town in the mountains of Tennessee.' That was all right with me but not—I discovered when I called home the next week—all right with my mother. She was literally reading Thessalonians to gather strength for how to deal with this slur on the family. 'We never thought of ourselves that way,' she said. 'You had a library card from the day you were three, and music lessons from the day you were four. You had everything you needed that was important.'

" 'Everything I needed that was important' included a grandfather who lived a few doors down the street. He was one of eighteen brothers and sisters. He ran away from home when he was eleven years old, eventually became a railroad engineer out west, but got back home to the mountains in time to sit on the porch and instruct me and the other children on Ruth Street,

'Aim for the top. There's more room there.' So we grew up believing we could be the railroad engineer, or the principal like my father, or a concert pianist, or the governor—or even the president of the United States. That was our picture of our future in this country. We never doubted it for a minute.

"When I walked to school, those four blocks were so filled with nosy neighbors interested in my well-being that I couldn't have gotten into much trouble even if there had been much trouble to get into.

"My teachers at Maryville High School taught me much more than algebra and English: the importance of the Pledge of Allegiance, of telling the truth, of where our civilization came from, to work and be on time, the difference between right and wrong."

"Sounds a lot like Aunt Liz," Fred said.

I said, "The Presbyterian church was across the street from the school. It seemed like the church was always open, and we were always there. Sunday morning, Sunday night fellowship, Monday night Scouts, Wednesday prayer meeting, Thursday choir practice. Sometimes I even played the piano at revival meetings while my father led the singing.

"When I was ten years old my father brought me to the courthouse one Saturday morning to meet our congressman. The congressman gave me a dime. I will never forget it. And when I left I was sure I had met the most respected man I was ever likely to meet, other than my father, my grandfather, and the preacher. I was taught to look up to the congressman and what he did.

"Fred, this is still the country of opportunity but a lot of people—especially young people—don't believe that anymore. There seem to be more and more people who can't imagine these opportunities for themselves in the same way I always have and you have, too. I believe it's mainly because not everyone grew up with the privileges we had. They didn't have 'everything they needed that was important.' And I believe those two things—confidence in your opportunities and those privileges—go hand in hand."

Then I asked Fred Montgomery, "What about you? Do you believe your grandchildren will have more opportunities growing up in this country than you have had?" Fred smiled and looked at Ernestine. "You know, for us, that's a question that requires a big answer. We have seven children, and twenty-four grandchildren, and now twenty-seven great-grandchildren. My answer is yes, I believe they will have—but only if we get back those values that we had before. These are the most important things," he said slowly.

There was an air of resignation in Fred's voice. "When I was a boy, the most ominous thing someone could say to you was 'The next time, I'm going to tell your dad.' When we came along, the whole community oversaw the growing up of young people. Now we can't do that. If you spank somebody else's child you're going to wind up in court. We can't go back to where we were,

13

and in many ways I wouldn't want to. But there is nothing to keep us from going back to the values we had. You can't hire enough policemen to do the job that parents are supposed to do."

It was 9:45 P.M. The firecrackers were popping and rockets were soaring high in the sky. The police chief and the teachers and the neighbor said good night and went home. I went to the guest room and prepared for bed, and I thought about this first day of our drive.

I thought, too, about a visit to Henning a year earlier. Our younger son, Will, and I had driven down to Memphis to the Southeastern Conference basketball tournament. Our teams lost early, so we came home early—and dropped by Henning to see the Haley Museum. Will and Alex had been friends, too. I can still see this friendly bear of a man cradling newborn Will in his arms when we first met in 1980. Alex was—at that moment—the world's most celebrated writer, and I was governor of his native state. *Roots* had won the Pulitzer Prize and was being translated into thirty-seven languages. The TV miniseries had become the most-watched program in history.

Alex was rich and famous and everyone seemed to know him. But what we liked most about him were his stories and his lessons. I believe Alex was put on earth to teach the lessons of *Roots* and left here for a while longer to remind us of some other important lessons. The Reverend Jesse Jackson said of Alex at his funeral, "He made our grandparents superstars." He also reminded us that these superstars came from super places that we often took for granted—our hometowns.

When Will and I made that visit to the Haley Museum, Fred Montgomery had given us the tour and talked about how the boys grew up. I remember his pointing and saying, "When Alex's grandpa came in, he sat here and we showed him some respect. When we sat at the foot of the steps listening to his grandma and aunt Liz rock and tell those stories, we never said a word. Children were to be seen and not heard.

"Our parents chose with whom we played. If a boy came by with trouble in his mind, Alex's mother would call us in and she might say to the boy, 'Aren't you late going somewhere?' and he might say, 'Yes ma'am,' and then she would say, 'Well, then, you'd better get on.' And only then, after he had left, were we permitted to go back outside."

I could tell, after a while, that all of Fred's conversation was being aimed directly at fifteen-year-old Will. "After nine P.M.," Fred went on, "if there was a boy and girl your age, Will, they never stayed alone in the same house together. It just wasn't done. And one more thing. At nine P.M. in every black home in Henning with which I was familiar, we went down on our knees in prayer because we believed that somehow our prayers would be lifted up into the clouds and that tomorrow would be better than today."

Mayor Fred Montgomery then looked directly at my son and said, "You know, Will, I know that must sound awfully old-fashioned to you, but it worked."

WE KNOW WHAT TO DO

✳

Before I went to sleep I made sure I had saved in a safe place the scrap of paper on which I had scribbled the words of the blessing that Fred Montgomery had said that evening before we ate our supper: "No matter how your ancestors arrived here, no matter what color your skin, no matter what language your grandparents spoke, we are all here. We are all Americans. And with all her faults, America is still the greatest place in this world to live. Cherish your country. Cherish your freedom and hold on to your dreams."

MISTY AND AARON GATES
PHOTOGRAPH BY CHUCK NICKLE

CHAPTER 2

Take This Job . . . Please

CASSVILLE, Missouri

They say they are angry, this young couple sitting across from me in the factory town of Cassville, in southwest Missouri. But the timbre in their voices isn't mean or resentful, it's just perplexed.

Misty is twenty-two and Aaron twenty-three. They have been married for nearly four years and both work at the Fasco Industries, making motors and blowers that go into air conditioners, ceiling fans, stoves, and copying machines all over the country and even in England. The company, in fact, is British-owned. "Isn't that something?" asked Aaron, one of those what's-wrong-with-this-picture kind of questions.

Both work six days a week at the factory, fifty hours or more, for less than nine dollars an hour, and hold down second jobs. They don't complain about it. Living costs are low and they believe in working hard, in doing all the things that are supposed to lead to that sacred slice of the American pie. They tithe (giving a percent of what they earn to their church). They've started an IRA. They have lived in an apartment and a small trailer and want their own home. Between them, Aaron and Misty make enough to pay their bills and put away a few dollars in savings. They can't afford the 20 percent down payment on a conventional mortgage, yet they make too much to qualify for an FHA home loan. When their application was rejected, a clerk told them flat out: "Either you both need to quit your jobs or one of you needs to get pregnant."

On the night we talked, they were talking about having a first child. Misty was worried. When she told her family of her plans, her great-grandmother asked, "Why, Misty? Why would you want to bring a baby into this world?"

And she knew that when she stopped working to have a child, she would lose her benefits—her seniority, her retirement plan, her two-week paid vacation. If and when she went back, she would have to start at point zero. Meanwhile, she and Aaron see some of their former schoolmates living together, having babies, unemployed. They don't marry, they don't work, because they don't want to lose their federal assistance, their welfare. They do not live in luxury, but they drive cars and rent or own houses that Misty and Aaron don't feel they can afford.

In all of our society, few issues are as vexing as welfare. Crime and acts of violence are primal and sometimes random. But the welfare system is a symbol of government's good intentions run amok. It discourages couples who want to marry, and too often penalizes those who want to work.

We cannot be heartless in looking at ways to reduce welfare or make it more efficient. We can't punish babies, the disabled, or the very elderly, who are the most vulnerable among us. But what we can do is put the decisions where they belong. In Cassville, and in every community that I visited on my drive, I was reminded that the people know who needs help and who doesn't, who works and who won't but could.

In the summer of '94, Fasco needed to hire three hundred new employees to get its regular shifts off overtime. George's chicken-processing plant, five miles down the road at Butterfield, had openings for two hundred. Tyson (chickens) and Justin (boots) each needed to fill one hundred jobs.

The jobs have gone begging. "Some people figure they are better off sitting at home," said Aaron, who once worked at George's but quit after a clash with one of his bosses. "A chicken plant isn't the perfect job," he added, "but it's not like people think. If you want to work, it's there. They interview you, they walk you through the plant, and pretty much tell you the same day the job is yours. Come back tomorrow."

Misty and Aaron are new members of our family. We acquired each other when Misty's mother, Lonna, married my first cousin Larry Mac Edens. This was the first marriage for Larry, who is fifty. He and Lonna live with his mother, my ninety-two-year-old great-aunt, Sula, in her farmhouse seven miles outside Cassville. I slept there for two nights in the room where my mother and grandmother were born and my grandparents were married.

Thirty years had passed since my last visit to Cassville, forty since I played there in the summers. I was always certain that my grandfather let the grass grow until my arrival. I cut it with a scythe in the hot sun.

I was nine or ten when I started spending my school vacations there. My grandfather Reu Rankin bought a farm near Cassville and retired to it after he left the railroad, ill with cancer of the larynx. His voice was a loud whisper, and to spare it he used a whistle to call his dog, Sandy. I still have that whistle. He was a towering figure, six feet six, and he had a creative side. He taught me how to type.

He wanted to submit a story to *Reader's Digest*, about a train wreck he had survived at Sapulpa, Oklahoma. The engine of the train jumped the track and he was pinned under it. He felt the spray of the water and for a suspenseful moment his fate hung on whether it was cold or steam. If it had turned out to be steam, he would have been a goner. He brought out his old Royal typewriter, showed me how to hit the keys, and had me type his words into a manuscript. I am not sure which of us was more excited when we put it in the mail. I no longer recall how many months we waited before we realized we were never going to hear from *Reader's Digest.*

Those were joyful summers for me. We drank raw milk and I learned that iced tea was meant to be served in generous glasses. The house where my grandmother was born in 1888, and my mother in 1914, sits on 110 acres of what was once choice farmland. Wheat was the main crop, and corn when there was moisture, but most of Cassville is cattle country now.

Electricity first came to the house in 1946, with a 100-watt light bulb hanging from the ceiling in each room. On that first night, no one went to bed. The family would sit there in the living room, just staring at each other under the bright light, looking into faces they had never seen so clearly after sundown.

They were in a world of constant newness, and they had a great sense of humor. Aunt Sula taught a canary to sing "The Sidewalks of New York." When her sister-in-law, Aunt Clara, died and her open casket was laid out in the family room, the canary wouldn't stop singing "The Sidewalks of New York." Sang all through the service. During my growing-up years, the relatives were always talking about how that canary wouldn't stop singing.

Aunt Sula has spent her life on this farm. She has had a hip replacement but moves faster on a walker than most of us do unassisted. Aunt Sula still has her perpetual good humor and her boundless capacity for work. When I visited years ago, before I was awake she would be gathering eggs, washing, hanging clothes, pumping water, cooking, and washing. Before lunch, she would hang the wet clothes. My most vivid memory of Cassville is Aunt Sula in the side yard about 11:00 A.M., chasing, catching, and wringing the neck of an unfortunate Rhode Island Red hen, who would then become a plateful of fried chicken and the centerpiece of a massive noon dinner.

Her husband, my great-uncle Floyd, who died in 1960, would have been at work milking well before daylight. He would come back in for a big breakfast fixed by Sula, sometimes running so as not to miss *Lum 'n' Abner* on the radio. And then, right back out on the tractor. He would return in time for the noon farm report and weather and the dinner spreading all over the table. Then he would lie down on the hard floor by the screen door, windows up, and take a short nap. Then he was back in the field until supper. After the sun went down, you would find him sitting in the yard, trying to catch the evening breeze. "There is almost always a breeze," Sula says.

I once asked Aunt Sula what else Floyd liked to do. There was a lengthy pause as she weighed the question. "Baseball," she said. "He would watch it on TV." "What else?" I asked. "Mainly," she said, "he worked."

They were not unusual for their time. They were part of a generation, born at the turn of the century, tested and tempered by two world wars and a depression, who lived off the land.

Larry always worked, too, and when I visited I worked with him—cutting hay, painting the barn, chasing cows. The farm has been in his family one hundred years, but there is not much profit in his kind of farming anymore. So Larry tends his cattle and works six hours a day at an old friend's construction company. His wife, Lonna, is in her seventeenth year at the motor and blower factory, where Misty and Aaron pull their shifts. Lonna's pay has topped out, or nearly so, at $10.45 an hour.

America lost something important when we lost this way of life. It gave us a whole set of principles and truths. For miles around, farmers would come to help a neighbor build a barn or put on a roof. They would help with the harvest, comfort one another when the hard times came. That was the rhythm of living then, and the way of dealing with tragedies that interrupt the rhythm of living. As we watch the people of Oklahoma City so courageously put their lives back together after that terrible blast, we are reminded that this is still the way America works best.

Larry tore down the barn in 1970. A tornado disabled the water pump in 1976. So I didn't wake up to the crowing of a rooster and Larry wasn't out milking.

For many that way of life is gone—2 percent of Americans are farmers today—but the values have been passed on to Misty and Aaron. They see a different set of values developing in Barry County, however, and they don't like it.

Both of my nights in Cassville, the two of them

dropped by, and it didn't take long before they were talking about their work, and welfare.

Misty described how she was buying groceries in Springfield one day, and a small, elderly lady in front of her tried to pay for dog food with food stamps. The cashier wouldn't let her, so she put the dog food away and tossed a couple of steaks and some hamburger meat into the cart. Then she told the cashier, "If I can't buy it with food stamps, my dog will eat steaks."

This wasn't one of those stories that have become a part of our folklore, about people on welfare climbing out of a Cadillac, or standing in line wearing $150 Air Jordans. Misty said she didn't resent an older lady getting food for stamps. "I care about pets. I just don't think they should eat better than we do," Misty said. She felt the indignation of a person who rarely works an eight-hour day. "It's fifty-six to sixty hours a week," she said. "I'm working all these hours and buying Always Save, the generic brand, and other people are sitting at home doing nothing."

She isn't just talking about strangers. Some of her former classmates are on welfare, as are people she worked with at Fasco. A young woman from her department was unmarried, expecting a baby, and seemingly unconcerned about who the father was. "She said she didn't care if she knew or not," said Misty, "because she can have her baby and sit at home and make more money than I do. She worked until the baby came."

The salt in the wound comes when her friend brags about not having to pay medical expenses for her baby.

"Even though I'm sitting here griping," she said, forcing a smile, "at least I'm working for what I have. That matters to me. It makes me feel a little bit better about myself. Someone isn't handing it to me. But it doesn't mean that it doesn't make me mad."

When you have seen your parents work hard just to pay their bills, and this is your ethic, it can be discouraging to see someone you know enjoying a free ride. You are tempted to think, as Misty said, "Why don't I just quit? My friend is on welfare, she has food stamps and Aid to Families with Dependent Children. Okay, the aid is supposed to buy things for the new baby. She is going to get this for the next eighteen years, at least, and her food stamps pay for every bit of her food. At one time, our next-door neighbor was getting almost two hundred dollars twice a month in food stamps. That's more than we spend. To me, that is just not right. They are getting everything free and we pay for everything we get."

On a typical day, Aaron and Misty are up each morning at three-thirty. Their first shift is at five, sometimes four, in the morning and they punch out at three-thirty in the afternoon, eleven to twelve hours later. They get thirty minutes for lunch with three ten-minute breaks. The benefits are decent: They pay only $6.00 a week for family health coverage. They invest 6 percent of what they make into a 401(K) retirement plan and the company puts in a matching amount. Aaron has been in

27

the plan for two years and has almost $2,000 saved up, money he can't touch.

They are modest people, this young couple, with modest dreams. They want to move out of their trailer and into a home of their own. They have been looking at a house priced at about $60,000. It bugs them both to know they have to surrender to the system to own a home. With an FHA loan, your monthly payments are based on your joint income and the number of people in your family. There is no down payment, so they can probably move in for the closing costs, around $1,000.

"What's probably going to happen," says Misty, "is that I will quit work just before I have a baby so we can qualify for the house. Then I'll go back to work. You can quit for a couple of months and still be eligible for the federal loan."

In a town the size of Cassville, Aaron has seen what he calls the family cycle of welfare. "There are people I graduated with," he says, "or would have graduated with if they had stayed in school, and it's the way they were raised. Their parents were on welfare and that's the way the kids know how to do it. The kids can quit school and the parents aren't going to lose any money from it."

I looked around the sturdy, two-story white frame house that Aunt Sula now owns, and my great-grandfather owned before her. Every board, every nail, spoke of toil and care. Great-grandpa Edens, Uncle Floyd, Larry Mac, now Aaron, they worked hard. That was all they knew. In another time, they worked outdoors, in the sun, and with age the backs of their necks looked like the lines on a map.

Aaron talked about how the cycle of welfare could be broken.

"They need to be told," he said, "that if your kid drops out of school, then you lose that child's money. And there needs to be a stipulation: If you are able to work, then you need to go out and try to get a job. We know couples who won't get married because they get two welfare checks, two sets of food stamps, and everything else. They are just living together because there is nothing they can do."

Misty spoke up. She knows a young woman in Cassville, a few years older, who has three kids. "She has child support, she's on welfare, plus she was baby-sitting until she got caught. She quit baby-sitting so she wouldn't lose her welfare checks. Now, Aaron and I looked at a 1993 Cougar when they first came out. I absolutely love them. This one had leather seats and our payment was going to be almost five hundred dollars a month. I couldn't afford that car. The next week, she went down there and bought one. She is on welfare and I'm out there working my butt off . . . and I was furious. I just thought, here I am working and you are driving *my* car.

"People do look down on someone like that," continued Misty, "and usually they get treated like dirt. People might have a little more respect for them if there was some legitimate reason they can't work. Then that's fine. There is a lady who is just barely Social Security age, and I saw her in a store on New Year's Day. She is getting like fourteen or fifteen dollars a month and that won't buy milk and bread and eggs. I feel real sorry for this lady because here she is, old enough to retire, and she's worked all her life."

I was in Cassville for two nights, and on the second one we all went to a dinner at the Roaring River State Park restaurant, where I spoke to about fifty Republicans. After dinner, I played the piano while Albert E. Brumley, Jr., the son of one of the great composers of gospel music, sang his father's most familiar tunes. Two of them were "I'll Fly Away" and "Turn Your Radio On." Albert senior wrote eight hundred songs at his home in the next county.

Later that night, Aaron and Misty dropped by the house so we could continue our talks. I asked Aaron what he wanted for his children. He thought about the question, and then said, "To not be ashamed to work for a living, for what they have. To learn responsibility. When my parents got divorced, I learned things don't always turn out the way you want. But my dad said, 'Nothing in life is handed to you. If you want something you will have to work to get it.' I worked out in the farm, and I worked all week and I got the weekend off. I got paid for the work I did. If you didn't work you didn't get paid. If you got into trouble or messed up, they cut your wages or you got fired.

"Going to church is a big thing. Basing your life in God. I mean, that's a big part of it. If you do that, bring your children up right, teach them the values you learned, then they are going to know right from wrong. But too many people think if you get into a bind, you can go on welfare. The government is there to bail you out. When I work fifty-six hours, I bring home around four hundred dollars, which I think is good."

Aaron works a second job in the fields, hauling hay. Misty loves to tell the story of how he saved enough to buy a used 1991 Thunderbird. "I know this sounds crazy," she said, although it didn't to me, not at all. "He had been wanting one forever. You talk about feeling good about earning it. They ran a credit check, and it made me feel really good when they came back and said, 'For your ages, you guys have got excellent credit.' We have really tried to keep our credit good."

Driving on to Oklahoma the next day, thinking about Cassville, it seemed to me that Uncle Floyd and Aunt Sula had it right. So did my grandfather, when he put me out there in the summer sun with the scythe before I could go fishing. So do Misty and Aaron. They understand how it ought to be. The first part of the promise of American life is that we are lucky enough to live in a country that we believe has an unlimited future. The second part is, that future is available to every one of us, no matter from where we might have come—if we will work. In three centuries, that simple notion has helped to create an ethic that helps to support the most remarkable country in the world. The problem is that today Misty and Aaron are surrounded by a kind of superstructure of misguided public policies that devalue that ethic.

31

Nothing makes Americans angrier, and almost nothing destroys our confidence in our future more, than what has happened with welfare. As this is being written, Washington is in the middle of trying to fix it one more time. I think Washington is making a mistake. Welfare can't be fixed in Washington, D.C. We've proved that, reinventing it six times since 1964. What we have gotten instead is more spending and more dependency. I don't believe new Republican rules from Washington, D.C., about welfare will be any better than old Democratic rules from Washington.

I believe we should send all the welfare decisions and money home—back to the states or, even better, back to the communities where people actually live and work. Cut Big Brother Washington out entirely. Not even "block grants" with Washington pulling the strings. Let the states and communities use the money as best they see fit. The states are already way ahead of Washington on requiring welfare recipients to get jobs and go to school and do community service, jailing deadbeat dads, and privatizing job-finding programs.

I have come to this conclusion: Whether it's altering the behavior of a welfare mother or a third grader, reinventing America in Washington, D.C., is a pipe dream. The bureaucracy is too strong. The interest groups are too nosy. There is too much difference between the way Washington works and the way people live.

The only way such matters can be worked through is state by state, neighborhood by neighborhood, family by family. "There is no need for there to be any unemployment in Cassville," Larry Mac says. "There are plenty of jobs." Misty and Aaron know who needs help—and who ought to get up and go to work. Let them and their neighbors make the decisions about welfare. They know what to do. That's remembering the American dream, not reinventing it.

FATHER JERRY HILL
PHOTOGRAPH BY EARL WARREN

CHAPTER 3

Homeless, Not Hopeless

DALLAS, Texas

Against a darkening night, the silhouette of the Dallas skyline is a dramatic sight but, as in many large American cities, something is wrong with the picture. Most residents of Dallas do not go downtown after dark except to attend a sports event or the occasional charity dinner. The rest, the ones who stay when the fun seekers leave, are the ones who have nowhere else to go.

Just before 8:00 P.M., I arrived at the Austin Street Shelter, where 208 homeless men were waiting for the Sai Babba, an Indian religious group, to serve the vegetarian meal these men received that night.

I had gone to that drab area of downtown Dallas to meet Father Jerry Hill, a priest whose black tunic and white collar blended nicely with his salt-and-pepper hair. He has none of the hard edge you might expect from one who, in his words, had been on the streets for twenty-two years, starting in Chicago. I had heard about his work from my sister Jane, whose husband is the preacher at the church that helped to start the shelter.

I, too, was hungry after a long drive from Oklahoma, and shared the supper of buttered bread, spaghetti and sauce, fresh green salad, milk, and a banana. On his way out, the Sai Babba leader stopped at Father Hill's seat and said, "Thank you for the opportunity you are giving us."

The shelter was built like a warehouse, with the stark, hollow feel of such places, but clean. The building is empty from six till eleven in the morning, so that it can be scrubbed from wall to wall. There are no handles on the outside of the doors, meaning they can be opened only from inside. The gate is part of a tall wire fence that surrounds the building and is locked at night.

The shelter is run entirely on private contributions. Father Hill won't accept government money. "When I was in Chicago," said Father Hill, "I would have to take off all of Friday to fill out the forms justifying what I had done Monday through Thursday to receive the grants.

"The most important rule I have," he continued, "is that no one is *entitled* to come into this shelter. If they're on drugs, they don't come in. I refuse to take them. If I have to hire a security guard to watch them, I don't want them. I've had to call the police only twice in the past year. It's rare to find a fight in here, even though you have up to three hundred men sleeping on pallets on the floor.

"Especially in the last two years, it has been unusual for anyone in their twenties or thirties to walk in who's not using crack. It's an epidemic. I've been working on the streets for twenty-two years and it shocks me.

"This population that I work with has been pushed out by crack users, back into the Dumpsters and the alleys where I found them years ago. I try to encourage a person who is homeless to become self-sufficient. Everybody groups the homeless into one category and they're not."

I sat with Father Hill at one of the long community dining tables and talked until the television set went off at 10:00 P.M. Many of the residents were already asleep. A few stayed at the tables, chatting in the dark, but the rest drifted away to claim their sleeping spaces. I stretched out on a blue mat. The overhead lights were off, but there was light at each end of the hall. Eight huge floor fans kept the air stirring and provided a nice, steady hum for sleeping.

No one needed a blanket on a warm July night in Dallas, but the temperature wasn't unpleasant. Everyone slept in his clothes, most without shirts. Possessions were wrapped neatly in plastic sacks or in old shirts, and used as a pillow. All ages and races were represented.

37

I rolled over several times during the night, but slept well. I was reminded of my friend Dwight McCarter, the back-country ranger in the Smoky Mountains, who sleeps by himself on the ground at night. He had become so used to this routine that when he went to his home in town he still slept on the floor. He said the bed hurt his back.

The hard floor was not so forgiving to my own back, and I was a little stiff when I woke up at about 4:30 A.M. Men were already sitting up on the pallets, milling around, talking quietly. There was the usual snorting and gurgling and nose-blowing and the other noises that accompany masses of people waking up in the morning. I was grateful for the steady, overriding hum of the floor fans.

At 4:45 the overhead lights came back on. At 5:00, volunteers from a Methodist church showed up to serve breakfast from hot vats. I don't believe Father Hill had slept much at all. Twice during the night he had to deal with emergencies. Just before midnight, a woman had come to the door with her two-year-old. She had been robbed and had a black eye and wanted to come in. Just before dawn, one of the older men complained of chest pains. In each case, Father Hill called 911 and ambulances took the two to Parkland General Hospital, the same hospital where President Kennedy was rushed after being shot in November 1963.

One night on the floor of a shelter wouldn't make me an expert, but I wanted a better understanding of why these two hundred men were there, and what it would take to get them on their feet. I already knew where to find the real experts—Father Hill on Austin Street and Jan Langbein, a few miles away at the Genesis women's shelter, whom I also visited while in Dallas.

The modern problem of the homeless is perhaps our most persistent reminder of how hard it is to come to terms with the different times in which we find ourselves. "The world changed in 1980," Father Hill once told me. "About the time Lone Star Steel downsized. I saw it in my shelters. Instead of men in their fifties, mostly white, usually alcoholic, the men coming in each night were in their thirties, of all races, out of work. The kind of manual-labor jobs they could handle disappeared and they couldn't fit back in."

I know that the phenomenon of the homeless is more complicated than that. Part of it is drugs. Part of it is the breakdown of the family, the natural support system. Part of it is the changes that occurred in state mental facilities in the 1970s and 1980s. We went too far with those and have left too many people on the street who genuinely need institutional help. But the real root cause of homelessness, I am convinced, is jobs.

Here is why I, too, believe the world changed in 1980 or thereabouts. I saw it from a different perch than Father Hill did from his shelters. I was governor of Tennessee at the time, worrying about how a state that was near the bottom in family incomes would cope with the onrush of what we were describing as the telecommunications age. As a state, we learned to cope very well and the things that worked best were: number one, creating an environment that would produce a steady stream of new jobs; number two, not counting on Washington to do for us what we should be doing for ourselves; and number three, recognizing that the strength of the family, the neighborhood, the church, and the school have everything to do with how solidly we can keep our feet on the ground in hard times. In other words, if a good job was available and if a person had the values that usually come from a good family and a good school, and especially if he or she had the moral core that usually comes from a strong religious base, then that person had almost everything he or she needed that was important to succeed.

Some people don't like to hear public figures say these things, but they are perfectly obvious, even though they seem to have been completely forgotten by some people.

Father Hill seemed constantly to be running into bureaucratic obstacles to helping the men he serves find and keep jobs. He motioned to a far corner of the room. "We have a step-up, job-rehab component back there [for those who want to sign up for trade courses]. In 1988 or '89, there were real good job-training programs in air conditioning and refrigeration, cable-TV installation, nurse's aides. I put fifteen to twenty people through that training—it takes about six months—and they all found work. None of them wound up back in here or on the street. Hospitals and nursing homes, they all need nurse's aides.

"We would sign them up, send them to the school, and do the counseling and support services. In all their wisdom, they cut out these training programs. I can show you a booklet right now, put out by the Dallas Industry Council, offering job retraining. It's all computers. How many people are you going to hire in your office as computer operators? That's total foolishness. I had a black man in here, about forty-two years old, from the hills of Arkansas. He read at about a fifth-grade level. So I was talking to him one day about what he would like to do with the rest of his life. He said, 'I'd really like to work in a nursing home. I've been raised around old people.'

"And he had been. He was really good helping out around here with the elderly. So I said, 'Gee, what a cinch. I'll get you into a nurse's aide program.' I called this industrial council and got him an application and he went down for an interview. He came back that afternoon and said they had turned him down. I asked him why and he said, 'They told me I can't read.'

"I knew that was wrong. He was reading the newspaper while I called them and raised hell. I said, 'Look, he can read. Not like a TV newscaster, but he can read.' They said, 'Maybe it was a mistake.' I sent him back a second time. And they rejected him again.

"I said, 'What reason did they gave this time?' He said, 'Father Hill, I can't read medical terms.' For God's sake, they made him read medical terms. He didn't know how to say 'osteoporosis.' I mean, why does he have to know a medical term when they need nurse's aides to put people in bed, turn them, wash them, and empty bedpans? They have their rules. They wouldn't take him. He is still on the street. Absolute nonsense. It is a boondoggle of unbelievable proportions."

I asked Father Hill: "You have more experience than most. You spend a lot of time trying to help them find jobs. What works best?"

He said, "I need training in everyday fields like brake repair. How many of these Brake-Chek places are there across the nation? Muffler shops? Train them for common car repairs, as painters, as mechanics, as plumbing assistants. If I could get the building across the street, I would hit up these brake shops and car-repair chains and Mr. Goodwrench to see if they would donate the equipment. I'd have that whole building set up for different areas of auto repair. Within a year, I would have twenty-five of these guys trained and back in the work force and they would not return to the street.

"Now, that may not seem like a big number to you, but you are dealing with addictions and depression and defeat, a numbness of the spirit. Put up five or ten of these places, in fifty cities, and you start to make a dent in the problem. It can give them a purpose for living, so they don't end up begging. These are jobs you can get here in Dallas, in Shreveport, in Des Moines, in Jersey City. It is a trade. It is pride."

Thinking about Cassville, where there were plenty of jobs, I asked if the residents had considered leaving Dallas and looking for jobs in a smaller town.

He shook his head no. "In their frame of mind, leaving here, they would feel trapped. It brings up a lot of memories of childhood. They don't see the small towns as having anything. If those jobs were there, and if we could give people like myself and my staff a chance to work with them, yes, they would adapt. But it would take time and support from social workers because this is the mentality they have. I'll give you an example.

"When I was on Chicago's skid row, I was working with a grandmother and her grandson, in the Cabrini Green housing project. He was sixteen years of age and heavily into drugs, just really screwing up his life. She was a good woman, the grandmother. She cared about this boy. She came to me one day and said she needed to do something or he was going to wind up dead or in prison. So I started quizzing her and I found out that she had inherited a little frame house in a small farming community in Mississippi. She owned it. I said, 'I'll buy the bus ticket if you can get your grandson back there and give him this space. If he gets out of Cabrini Green, he has a chance to retrieve his life.'

"She looked at me like I was a damned fool, like, 'What do you mean? Let him go back to the rural South? No way.' She would not even consider it. I witnessed then the frame of mind, this stubbornness. In some small country towns they have as much of a homeless or poverty problem as the major cities. You can save some of the people if they would make the transition, but they won't do it on their own."

These local problems are hard enough, but the government makes it worse. "The most damaging thing now, and if it doesn't change it will only get worse, is opening up Social Security benefits to allow for drug addiction," says Father Hill. "I am telling you, every punk on the street that's on crack or anything else wants to draw Social Security. I had an argument with two caseworkers this week. The addict comes in, wants to see the psychiatrist, they are depressed and they are this and that. So the psychiatrist writes down, 'Yes, they are disabled as a result of being addicted,' and they can get on SSI. When that happens, I can kiss them good-bye because they lose all motivation. They get four hundred and forty-six dollars a month, and once they get on that they have absolutely no desire to do anything for the rest of their lives. What we are doing is supplementing drug use. I have spent my whole ministry getting people motivated to go back into society. And this is killing them.

"It has been going on for the past two or three years. I have a lot of critics on this, but at the present time anyone under forty who gets on SSI, I throw them out of the shelter. There is nothing else I can do with them. I can't motivate them. They just lose it."

*

We were met at Genesis House, a residential facility for battered women and their children, by the director, Jan Langbein. She described how they started in the First Presbyterian Church, the one where my sister's husband, Bill, is the preacher. "Father Hill was working ecumenically with the Stewpot Ministry," she said. "He came across a woman who was basically living out of her car because it wasn't safe for her to live at home. She wasn't your typical street woman. So when he began talking to her, and finding out what her needs were, he found that she had been abused and battered. When he tried to find a safe home for her, the nearest place was in Jacksonville, Florida.

"Now this was in 1982. The need was there. As Austin Street grew out of that basement, our people said, 'It is not okay to live under a bridge. It is not okay to live in your car because your home is unsafe.' This was how it started. As they began to look for space, everyone had the attitude, this is a fine idea but not in my backyard.

"When I looked for outreach office space within the last two years, I kept hearing landlords say, 'We don't want you here. We don't want bums here.' I'm not sure which bums they were talking about. I think people have a preconceived idea of who is battered in this country and we want to think they look like somebody else. We want to think it is an ethnic group or an economic group, other than our group. But they look like me. As you walk through here, some of the people that you pass are residents. Some are staff. And other than me, because I am the only one who wears hose and heels, and I do that because I'm always calling on contributors, you are hard-pressed to guess who lives here and who works here."

The building was an old abandoned firehouse in Oak Cliff, leased from the city of Dallas for a dollar a year. Those first few months it must have been a clear case of rent gouging, but they performed wonders. They created a very homelike environment, with living quarters upstairs, bedrooms, bathrooms, living and dining rooms.

"We are here for whatever their needs are," said Jan. "Some women stay twenty minutes, some stay twenty days. We try to limit the stay to two weeks, but while they are here we are working on whatever they need. If a husband or boyfriend harasses them on the job, we get a restraining order. If he knocked out some teeth, we arrange for dental work. We get their eyeglasses replaced. Jackets for the kids. We had a wife who came in yesterday who literally snatched up her children in their pajamas. So we often start from scratch."

Jan has known socially some of the women who show up seeking help. "I am sometimes amazed at who comes here," she said. "I am constantly amazed by the creativity with which one person will abuse another. I thought it was going to be a split lip and a black eye. The abuse is incredible. Just when I think I have heard it all, something new turns up. Because there are just sixty safe beds for battered women in a city the size of Dallas, we operate at full capacity most always. Admission has to be based on how potentially lethal the abuse is. We do see the worst of the worst.

"The batterers know where to hit them so it doesn't show, or in a place where the woman would not reveal it—the cuff of the head or between the waist and the knees, these are the popular spots. The children come here clinging to their moms or lashing out at the world for what has been done to them. They are bed wetters and nail biters. They have nightmares about murderers with hooks for hands and knives dripping with blood. Those are the immediate manifestations of what they have experienced and what they have witnessed. And emotional abuse is at epidemic proportions. The saddest part is knowing that many of these true victims of violent homes will grow up to be the future abusers."

Jan has been trained as a social worker. She started with Genesis House as a volunteer and was promoted to executive director. Her passion just drills you. We not only haven't known how to end domestic violence, for far too long we haven't known where to begin.

Jan told the story of a nine-year-old boy who wouldn't eat in the dining room. A caseworker had a plate prepared and told him to take it to his room. Later, she explained to Jan: "He is scared about being here. Plus, he has a burn scar on his neck and he's very embarrassed about that." Jan tried to comfort him by letting him know that the scars on the outside don't matter. She wanted to heal the scars on the inside.

We Know What to Do

When she put her arms around him, she felt the scar tissue that covered forty-five percent of his body. When he was seven, he had set himself on fire because of what had been done to him.

"This little guy will never be able to shed the problem," she said. "Within twenty-four hours of being in my shelter, he beat up another child. Within forty-eight hours, he had assaulted his teacher in school. I think about this little kid at night. I ask God to bless all these children. I think this is how we create serial killers. My hope is to break the cycle that is passed from one generation to the next. I hope that we can let these kids know that no one can hurt them here. To us, hitting your child for not eating green beans is no different than dad hitting mom for fixing green beans. And that is what we hear. I have never heard a woman say he beat me because he lacks conflict-resolution skills. He beat her because there wasn't cold beer in the icebox, because the potatoes weren't cut right, because she fried the chicken instead of baking it."

✳

Jan knows right where to put the responsibility for the results of the outrageous behavior she sees every day. "I know you are asking as you go around the country, what's the big problem here? and I think probably ninety-nine percent will tell you it is violence. We are sick of not being safe in our homes. We are sick of not being safe on the streets. It's gangs, but we are realizing that it doesn't start in the streets. It starts in our homes and spills into the streets. We can have laws and rhetoric and gang-prevention programs, but it all goes back to the home. When the kids see violence in the home, and it is reinforced on TV and in our music, our advertising, what can we expect?"

＊

There are also some clear lessons from Father Hill's experiences. To begin with, the government in Washington should stop giving drug addicts $446 per month to support their habit and thereby undermine everything Father Hill is trying to do to help them build up a sense of responsibility for themselves. Second, since what most of the men want is a job, I would take the $25 billion Washington spends on job training and turn it into vouchers for people like those in the shelter who want to work, or for anyone changing jobs or out of work. Let them take the voucher to someone who needs workers and say, "Here's the money. Now, in exchange, please train me." The best training for work is work. That would help get the federal and local bureaucracy out of the way. Third, whatever other money the government has to spend helping people back up on their feet, why not give it to people like Jerry Hill without a lot of rules and regulations? He obviously knows what to do and is doing it—but we have set up such a complicated system of federal government support for his efforts that he would rather raise the money privately than wrestle with the rules and regulations that come with the government money.

The clearest lesson of Father Hill's work is that in the end, it is not a distant government that can or should help the men who sleep in his shelter. That is first and foremost the responsibility, in this case, of the citizens of Dallas. And churches are a good place to start.

My brother-in-law Bill Carl's church, which helped start both Father Hill's and Jan Langbein's shelters, runs the largest social-ministries program of any downtown church in America. This includes a soup kitchen for the hungry and the only free dental care in the city. The church also helped start a housing coalition that finds houses for people in trouble, feeds and helps them for three months to organize their lives, and then, in Bill's words, kicks them out. "Our objective is to help them get back on their own two feet. At least two thirds of them make it.

"It has always been the Judeo-Christian tradition that the community takes care of its own," Bill says. "Only in this century has the community relinquished its responsibility to government. Matthew 25:35 is the basic text: 'I was a stranger and you took me in.' Our church publication is called 'Inasmuch'—'Inasmuch as you have done it unto the least of these, you have done it unto me.' That's from Matthew 25:40. The two great commandments of our religion, almost every religion, are 'Love God' and 'Love Your Neighbor.' 'Love Your Neighbor' literally means caring for those in the community."

Bill and I end up in about the same place although

coming from two different perspectives, his theological and mine political. Of course there are some things for the government to do and some changes we can make in the way government does these things. But the real solutions for the troubles found in Father Hill's and Jan Langbein's shelters begin and end in the homes, neighborhoods, religious institutions, and schools of every community in America.

ELLIS CORMIER
PHOTOGRAPH BY EARL WARREN

CHAPTER 4

Cajun Capitalism

JENNINGS, Louisiana

Our red Explorer sped along Interstate 10 through the marshes of South Louisiana. It was 7:20 P.M. and we were running late.

I knew we were nearing Jennings when I saw the billboard advertising the Boudin King restaurant, featuring "Louisiana spice at a good price." The sign said to take Exit 26, drive south for two miles, and turn right.

We had traveled south and east out of Dallas, through Houston and Beaumont. I had a date with a family whose entire history had been in small business and who lives by the belief you can do well for yourself

53

if you are persistent, resilient, resourceful, and stubborn.

This was the land of south Louisiana, not far from Evangeline, where the first oil well was drilled in the South. This is blue bayou country, with thickets of pine trees and live oak and short winters. The shortness of the winter months was once more significant than the scenery. In the days before refrigeration, boudin, the favorite food of the region, the end result of hog butchering, could occur only when the weather was cold.

Pronounced "BOO-dan"—you swallow the "n"—the dish is a Cajun delicacy best described as what is left of the hog after the sausage is made. It is created by combining rice and pork, the staple crop and meat of rural southern France, with kidney, spleen, green onions and parsley, all well seasoned, in a sausage casing.

"The *natural* casing. It sounds better than intestines," explained Ellis Cormier, the man known as "The Boudin King." Of his first-time customers, he added: "If I can get it past their eyes, I have them hooked for life."

Ellis is a Cajun, descended from the early French residents of Acadia (as parts of Nova Scotia and New Brunswick were once known), who were driven into exile by the British in 1775. Many of them made their way to the open spaces of Louisiana's marshes and swamps east of New Orleans.

The four favorite public sports in Louisiana are food, jazz, politics, and football. The food is spicy, the jazz hot, the politics magnificently twisted, and the football treated as a religious experience. All of these are somewhat interchangeable. I have my own Louisiana references. I made my first trip to Baton Rouge with the Vanderbilt University track team in 1959. On the way down we thought we had a pretty good 440 relay team. When we got there Billy Cannon and his teammates ran us into the ground. Cannon was that rare combination, an athlete with football speed and a shot-putter's strength. He won the Heisman Trophy that year.

In 1965, I came to New Orleans to clerk for Judge John Minor Wisdom, who sat on the court that ordered Governor Ross Barnett to admit the first black student to Ole Miss. At night I played the trombone and washboard in a Dixieland band at a place called "Your Father's Moustache" in the French Quarter. You could walk up any block and hear the music of Al Hirt, Pete Fountain, and the ageless jazzmen of Preservation Hall. Cotton, rice, shipping, and oil created the great fortunes of Louisiana, but the small businesses—the bars, shops, antique stores, the cafés and art galleries—are where the adventure is.

The French influence gives Louisiana its texture, and the legacy of Huey Long gives it intrigue. His brother, Earl, and his son, Russell, carried on the family dynasty for forty or fifty years. The assassination of Huey Long, the populist known as "the Kingfish," made him a legend in the state he served as governor and senator. He put the people back to work by rebuilding the roads and bridges, the completion of each marked by a plaque attesting to Huey's leadership. The roads and bridges are in decline now, but the plaques have held up well.

There is a story about Huey Long bursting into the Senate cloakroom in 1932, when the Bonus Marchers were advancing on Washington. His hair was askew and his eyes were wild. "Fellows," he said, "there's a mob in the streets. I'm trying to make up my mind whether to stay with you and defend this Capitol, or go out there and lead them against you."

In Jennings, and across Louisiana, many share that ambivalence about their government.

A state legislator once earned the wrath of Ellis Cormier by passing a proclamation that named the town of Broussard the "Boudin Capital of the World." The representative from Ellis's district, Jimmy Horton, had a flat tire that day and missed the vote. "Jimmy wouldn't have stood for it," said Ellis. "He would have fought. So we had to call Jennings something bigger than that, and he came up with a proclamation that made Jennings the 'Boudin Capital of the Universe.'" The Boudin King sees nothing unusual about this claim, or this form of intramural political dueling. He rather likes the title: "We can prove it is, you see. It would be good food to take up in space."

His recipe for boudin has been handed down from father to son for generations. His father started selling it out of a grocery the family opened during Franklin Roosevelt's last term as president. Ellis went to work in the family store after his discharge from the navy as an aviation mechanic. "Then after Daddy died," he says, "I decided I needed to close the grocery and go into the restaurant business with boudin as a main dish."

Ellis and June, his wife of fifty-two years, remember what the word around town was: that the restaurant wouldn't last two weeks. They had two strikes against them: They were closed on Sunday and they didn't sell liquor.

They have been in the restaurant business for twenty years now and they still don't sell beer or liquor. When their sales climbed to a ton of boudin a week, Ellis marked the occasion by running an ad in the local paper that said, "Thanks a ton." Now they have moved up to six thousand pounds (three tons a week) at the restaurant in Jennings and another in Crowley. Receipts for the previous week had totaled $20,500. It doesn't take a math major to figure out that they gross over a million dollars a year. This is a Cajun capitalist.

When the red Explorer pulled into a parking space, the whole clan was waiting for us. It was a family business in fact as well as in spirit. Two sons-in-law, Tom and Wendell, help grind out the boudin and one grandson, Randy McClure, works there when he isn't in school. Randy was planning to enroll in the engineering school at LSU in the fall.

The restaurant is rustic, with two dining rooms, a large one in back added on to the original grocery. Stuffed fish are mounted on the walls. The customers keep coming back, and the tourists pull off the freeway, because the food is zesty and the prices are a throw-

back to the 1950s. The sign outside promoted the daily
special: FRIED GIZZARD DINNER—$2.95. The boudin
goes for $2.15 a pound, mild or spicy, cooked, cold, or
frozen. You can order a seafood platter for $5.50, a
bowl of shrimp gumbo for $4.95, and a four-piece
chicken dinner for $3.79.

"We make boo-dan," said June. "Beautiful. We don't
ship it out. We don't wholesale it. You want it, you
come get it. We're not conceited. We just know we
make the best. No liquor. We're not open on Sunday.
About seventy-five percent of what we sell is at the take-
out window."

Ellis says a piece of advice from an uncle changed
his life. "We were still in the grocery business at the
time," he says. "We were struggling, not making a living. I'll tell you, I was in debt. My uncle came in one
day from Lake Charles. He had grocery stores there
and had gotten wealthy. I think they paid somewhere
around a half-million dollars in inheritance taxes when
he died. He made a lot of money. That's another thing
I learned from him. If you don't enjoy life while you're
living, Uncle Sam is going to take it away from you.

"He walked through the aisles and said, 'Ellis, I'm
going to tell you something that maybe you can use.'
He picked an item off a shelf and he said, 'Ellis, this is
too high.' He kept walking and he kept picking up cans
and boxes and each time he said, 'This is too high.'

"I said, 'What do you mean?' And he answered, 'Just
what I said. Number one, the prices are too high. Num-

ber two, nothing happens until a sale is made. Number three, you don't make a penny if something sits on your shelf. You don't make a penny on what your competitor down the street sells. One hundred percent of nothing is nothing.'"

Ellis leaned closer, as people tend to do when they are passing on eternal truths. "If the American people could learn those three statements," he said, "and all of us settle for less, we would have less taxes, too. We could compete with other countries, instead of having to support them."

I took out my pad and began scribbling notes, as I often do. Some people appear uneasy when I do this, but it just encouraged Ellis. I asked him to tell me about being a small businessman in the 1990s. Is it easier or harder today?

"It's harder," he said, without hesitation. "We have too much government and not enough responsibility. You never know what the next rule is going to be. Maybe I'm just a little tired, but that's the way I feel. The government just controls us too much."

"Sometimes I need a soapbox for him," June said, smiling.

"I sent a telegram once to Lady Bird Johnson," he said, "when she had that beautify America campaign. I told her those signs on the highway didn't unbeautify America. Some were unsightly, but my complaint was that little businessmen couldn't get the space, or couldn't afford 'em if they did. That was the last telegram I ever sent. I calmed down after that. Never heard back from Lady Bird. But I did get audited by the IRS a few weeks later. Had to hire a CPA."

Ellis is a rotund man with tattoos on his arms. He is full-faced and his eyes are bright, making his stare even more intense. "I'm a red-blooded American," he said. "I remember when America was great, a lot better than it is today. Of course, I have a lot more today than I did after the war. Nobody had anything then and the country wasn't in debt. Our government owes more money today than we can ever repay."

The Boudin King didn't have to fumble for words to pick out what was right with the country. "Freedom," he said. "We still have some. And you can make a good living if you want to work. You can go to the church of your choice. Some things are better. We have more good roads, better cars, jet travel. It's easier to get around. We have more pollution than we had. With industry it would be almost impossible to eliminate it, but I think it should be controlled more. They [the government] put some locks in the rivers near here to keep the salt water out of the rice, and we haven't had any clear water since then."

Ellis calls himself a real conservative—"People around here say I start where Rush Limbaugh stops"— and he doesn't think the country has been the same since we went off the gold standard. He employs twenty-five people in his restaurant, treats them with respect, and has little turnover. He doesn't want any part of a national health-insurance plan.

"I don't believe in the government having too much control," he said. "We have the greatest country in the world, but just a bunch of idiots running it. I think you have to educate people, teach them to compete."

Ellis is truly a red-blooded Cajun capitalist, an American original. I wouldn't try to persuade you that there is more than one Boudin King. But you don't have to drive very far across this country to find example after example of entrepreneurs with the spirit of The Boudin King, the kind you can't keep down, who find their way around every obstacle. And he has had his share.

June spoke up and said, "When Wal-Mart came in, all the smaller stores, TG and Y and Murphy's and some others, they just closed. Instead of fighting them, they closed."

Converting his grocery into a restaurant must have seemed a logical step. They had sold boudin in the grocery for many years. His mother made it in a tub at home. ("Don't write *tub*," said Ellis. "*Pan* sounds better.") Father and son brought it through the back door. I guessed that the big grocery chains had moved in on him, but he said no, that wasn't what put him out of business. Petty theft drove him out. "The first thing I knew," he said, "I'd be out of most of the stuff on the shelves and I'd restock and it would start over again. Then it was just hard times."

There is still theft in the restaurant, but of a kind that doesn't affect his cash flow. Someone stole an autographed photo of Cindi Lauper, the singer, right off his wall. She and her band had stopped one day for lunch and posed with Ellis. "Right off the wall," he said. "Why would you want someone else's picture of Cindi Lauper?"

Then the change jar for leukemia research disappeared. "It was next to the register," said June, "with the lid taped to the jar. They just walked out with it, a whole jar full of money. That's so sad."

We ate dinner as we talked. I ordered the shrimp gumbo, fried okra, hush puppies, cole slaw, fried oysters, and fried shrimp. I passed up the fried crawfish tails, the armadillo stew, and hogshead cheese.

"You know what a Cajun zoo is?" asked The Boudin King. "On each cage they have the name of the animal, the Latin name, and the recipe."

His own eating habits had undergone a recent dramatic change. Eleven weeks earlier, he had suffered a heart attack on a Tuesday night. He went to work the next day and it was Friday before June could check him into the hospital. He had bypass surgery on five arteries. "He was ninety percent blocked," said June. "We almost lost him."

"I'm a different man now," he said. "I do my exercises and I take a thirty-minute walk." He ordered a small green salad . . . and a few fried oysters. "Just for tonight," he said, with a wink.

The mayor and his wife had joined us, and the pride in their town was as thick as the gumbo. Jennings has twelve thousand people, forty-one churches, and three bars. "This is real Cajun country," said the mayor's wife. "Prairie Cajun. The swamp Cajun country isn't far away. Those are more like the Tennessee mountain men where you come from—loners."

When we finished dinner, and rose to leave, the mayor's wife said, "We say two things, *adieu,* which means 'go with God,' and *au revoir,* which means 'until we meet again.'"

Ellis lives on the block where he was born. I spent the night in his home, which had comfortable chairs, thick rugs, needlework everywhere, vases with artificial flowers, books, piles of videotapes, and exercise equipment. The Cormiers built the front part with a $10,000 loan, all the bank would give them, paid it off, and then took out another loan to finish the rest of the house.

These are salt-of-the-earth people, the kind who build their own business, work hard, and weather the rough times. They know what they believe in, what they came from, who they are. They are entrepreneurs and capitalists, and in America, they are the rule rather than the exception. And the number is growing, out of necessity. Perhaps 10 percent of the 100 million Americans who work in the private sector lose their jobs *every year,* as corporations downsize, big companies squeeze little stores, world competition increases, and we move further into the age of telecommunications. Government statistics may say that the economy is getting better, but on most mornings the average American driving to work wonders whether he will have a job when he gets there.

As Americans look for new jobs to replace those that

disappear, more and more of us are going to work for ourselves—like The Boudin King and June and their family. In the United States today, the private sector has more business owners than union members. In this way we are becoming a nation of shopkeepers—computer-age shopkeepers—with many people working at home, many with part-time jobs, more families working together. The work is different, but the workplace in many places is becoming more like the nineteenth century, when families farmed together, than like the twentieth century, when we organized ourselves into highly structured corporations.

There are about 240,000 fast-growing companies in America that create almost all of the millions of new jobs each year that we need to keep our standard of living high. More of them are like The Boudin King's restaurant than like General Motors. Keeping an environment in which Cajun capitalists can grow the largest number of good new jobs is the surest way to make sure America moves into the next century with a head of steam.

The first light was at 6:15 the next morning, and Ellis and I started walking along Dove Street, near the house his father built with his own hands. The homes were one-story, square and rectangular, neat, many with aluminum siding, some with a statue of the Virgin Mary in the yard. Air-conditioning units poked out of the windows. In the driveways were parked Chevy and

Ford trucks. On a few of the lawns, the SUPPORT THE TROOPS signs hadn't been taken down.

The weather was muggy and the bugs were feasting on my legs. As we walked, Ellis asked, "What are you going to do with that notebook?"

"I'm not sure," I said. "When I take notes it helps me to listen and to remember what I've heard and to think about it. I might write a book, but writing a book is hard."

He nodded. "I want to write a book one day," he said. "I'm going to call it *The Christian Hypnotist*. There is going to be a chapter against reincarnation, some chapters on some of the things I've done. I'm a hypnotist. I'm going up to New Hampshire for a convention in a couple of weeks. You know, most preachers are against hypnosis. They call it witchcraft."

Ellis was climbing back on his soapbox. "This country is going straight to the dogs," he said. "But, my God, it is a great country!"

He eyed me suspiciously.

"Are you a conservative, or a medium?" asked Ellis. "I won't even ask if you are a liberal."

"A conservative," I said. "Not one of those Washington conservatives. I was a populist, conservative Tennessee governor."

We finished our morning walk, which took us past the Jennings Full Gospel Worship Center, across the street from the South Central Bell Service Center. We passed the Bubba Ostalet Sales Center, which in other places would be called a used-car lot. After breakfast,

Ellis Cormier stood in his door, with his wife, June, and his daughter Linda, and waved us off. *"Adieu,"* he said, "and *au revoir."*

Louisiana is so hot in late July that the leaves appear to be wilting in the sun. The interstate highways are built high over the marshes, and the rains come so often and hard that you can't take the drive for granted.

Shortly before noon, we pulled into Baton Rouge, where I was to be the speaker at a luncheon. I was sitting with Doug Moreau, the district attorney for East Baton Rouge Parish, and he was explaining his objection to the new federal crime bill. "It's a problem," he said, "because if you take the money the first year it might not be there the third. Plus they don't know what fits. It would be like somebody in Washington cooking this lunch. By the time it got here, it would be cold and everybody would be gone."

I used his line in my talk. The crowd responded with an appreciative laugh. I think it would have gone over big with The Boo-dan King, too.

THE REVEREND HENRY DELANEY
PHOTOGRAPH BY EARL WARREN

CHAPTER 5

The Preacher Cracks Down on Drugs

SAVANNAH, Georgia

When he is invited to appear as guest preacher, the Reverend Henry Delaney is often advertised as "500 Pounds of Prophecy." He is in fact a huge and arresting black-robed presence, with a hearty voice and laugh, and a handsome face with the barely visible slit of a scar down his left cheek that you know didn't come from shaving. He could pass for George Foreman's larger, slightly older brother, with a wisp of white hair, dark eyebrows, and a lively mind filled with bits and pieces of history.

But his formidable appearance isn't all that makes Henry Delaney special. He is the answer to one of the questions I am constantly asked: If you roll back the federal government, then who is going to do what needs to be done? Henry Delaney, that's who. He already has. He has reminded us how to confront the drug plague and shut down the crack houses. He did it with faith and commerce and mostly private funding.

So this is about the scourge of drugs and a black preacher in Savannah, Georgia, who would not take no for an answer. He achieved dramatic results without millions in federal aid, and without trampling anyone's rights. Henry moved to one of the poorest sections of Savannah in 1989. His previous ministry had been in Detroit, and it was in his church that Hosea Williams and Ralph Abernathy became the first prominent black civil rights leaders to endorse Ronald Reagan in 1980.

Savannah is a graceful city of the Old South, the oldest settlement in Georgia. The first steamship to cross the Atlantic left from there and landed at Liverpool. This was where Eli Whitney's cotton gin began and General Sherman's march to the sea ended.

It's fair to say that a lesser person would have been daunted by what Reverend Delaney found in Savannah. He moved into a house on Thirty-second Street that had been boarded up and occupied by crack addicts. He inherited a ramshackle church, whose property was about to be foreclosed by the Department of Housing and Urban Development (HUD). His congregation consisted of 216 members, many of whom were afraid to attend church because of the drug dealers who overran the area.

Henry called the head of the local HUD office, a Reagan appointee. The reverend told him he was the "token Republican" on the block, new in town, and needed time to catch up. The deadline was extended.

Next, a group of black preachers decided to meet at St. Paul's, Delaney's church, to discuss which candidates to support for the school board. Henry told his story. Two days later, the president of the community's largest black-owned bank came to the back door of his church and asked if he could help.

"I told him," said Delaney, "that I needed a loan so we could start buying up the houses where the drug dealers lived. We bought five of them on one side of the street, and eight in the next block. As we kicked out the drug dealers, I started moving in my preachers."

His wife, Ethel, helped him repair the church and the members of the congregation pitched in to renovate the houses. With every house they overhauled, they expanded their drug-free zone. The church activities expanded and the membership leaped to three thousand members. Delaney now has sixteen ministers of the gospel, all of whom live within two blocks of the church.

His converts included some of the very dealers he had evicted. One was shot sixteen times when he was caught in the crossfire from a drug deal gone bad at a car wash. He made a miraculous recovery and now he never misses a Sunday morning service. They say that no one in the congregation sings "Amazing Grace" with more feeling.

Nothing seems to daunt Henry Delaney—not drug

lords, white society, or even marriage to a woman with five children. He was still preaching in Detroit when a cousin kept trying to arrange for him to meet Ethel. "Just what he needed, right?" she said. "But his cousin explained that four of the children were grown. I just had one child at home and that was Keith. Then he said, 'Okay, I'll meet her.' We were introduced at a revival in Nashville and four months later we were married."

Ethel had been a lab technician at St. Thomas Hospital in Nashville, had worked for twenty-five years, and owned a five-bedroom colonial house, where her daughter's family now lives. "When we married," she says, "Henry told me that I didn't have to work anymore. I asked him if he would repeat that, please. I don't know how I could work and do all the things we're doing."

I had been told that Henry Delaney was a black evangelist in the noblest tradition, a powerful orator, able to keep an audience riveted for an hour or more, a man of gifts. "He can preach hellfire like you never heard before," a lawyer told me. "This guy will mesmerize you when he really gets cooking. He is dynamic out there. He truly is."

Henry began by building a strong Bible study program, with two sessions every Tuesday. It turned into the largest Bible study group in the area, white or black. "Tuesday we had three hundred and eighteen for the one P.M. study," he said, "and nearly eight hundred at seven P.M. A lot of them come from other churches. The police let us double-park."

Whatever dropped into the box, and whatever he could borrow, went into buying up more real estate. The drug dealers gladly took their money and moved out, unwilling to challenge the zeal and growing influence of the mammoth minister. When the city of Savannah put a dilapidated school building up for sale, Henry snapped it up.

"It's five blocks away," he said. "We fixed it up and reopened as an all-boys school. Last year, our first year, we had sixth, seventh, and eighth graders, thirty-five boys, all of them 'at risk' students." They lost five who had behavioral disorders so severe they couldn't be controlled. "We are not a reformatory," said Henry. "We graduated six from the eighth grade. The tuition is two thousand dollars a year. We arranged to get some scholarship money for them, but everybody has to pay something."

He is educating inner-city kids in Savannah who otherwise would not be in school, who would drop out, be rejected or expelled.

So Reverend Delaney does it his way, tapping every source he can. In 1994, his budget for the school was $170,000, with several of his teachers volunteering their time. He went into the wealthiest community in Savannah, The Landings, and arranged a speech to the Kiwanis Club. "Most of the millionaires live out there," he said bluntly. "When they introduced me, I made sure to mention that I was a part of the Wayne County Republicans. That got their attention pretty good. One of the members asked our choir to come back and do a concert and we raised thirteen thousand dollars that night.

"Another fellow started teaching the boys chess, and one of the ladies is teaching manners at my wife's school—how to use napkins and all the rest."

Ethel Delaney meanwhile opened the St. Paul's Community Cultural Center—what she calls a Christian charm school for girls. Since they don't accept federal money, both schools instill a heavy dose of discipline and religion. Ethel—a fine musician and talented singer—teaches what she calls "praise dancing" to a class of thirty-four girls, ages five to sixteen. She puts on a tape of spiritual music, and "instead of the energy going the other way, we do praisercize instead of Jazzercise. Most of the dances are geared more toward praise, or worship, than the other type of thing. At the end of the year, we have a dance recital. They have to say a Bible verse when they come to get their diplomas."

*

Invited to the White House by the Reagans in 1982, Henry met Elizabeth Dole, and she told him about the Second Harvest food program. In Savannah, he and his wife got involved in this self-help network. "Last month," he said, "we were able to give bags of groceries to over four hundred families. We do it every month.

Each Sunday morning we have a breakfast for the homeless and one of our staff ministers to them. On Tuesday and Thursday we have what is called a kids' café. The chefs in the community send the food over— we pay eighteen cents a pound for it through Second Harvest—and the children come in between four P.M. and six P.M. and get fed." That day the café had served seventy-one kids.

Henry also runs a homeless shelter for young men who are recovering drug addicts and recent parolees from prison, helping them find jobs and keeping them clean from drugs. Twelve were in the program at the time I was there. I suppose much of what he does is also done at shelters in Dallas and Los Angeles and elsewhere. What is different is the evangelistic fervor he brings to the task. "Many of these fellows have gone through those twenty-eight-day detox programs, but within four or five days they are back at it."

So three nights a week, Monday, Wednesday, and Friday, he keeps them busy with evening worship. On Tuesday they have Bible study. On Sunday they attend regular church services. "So far," says Henry, "it has worked very well. Our rate is real high; eighty percent of these guys have been able to stay off the stuff."

He calls his shelter the Hallelujah House. This is how you have to conduct a war against drugs, using a series of trenches. It starts in the family. If you fail there, the school becomes your barricade. Lose them there, and you have to take them off the street and reassemble them for the workplace.

Of all the uphill battles he and his wife wage, Henry is most perplexed by the nation's failure to focus consistently on the drug issue. His is a voice from the inner city of Savannah that we should be listening to. In the 1970s, when national voices suggested marijuana was cool and drugs were okay, kids used drugs. In the early 1980s, when the national leadership and some in the media said it wasn't okay, drug use began to decrease.

But Henry Delaney knows that what he does at his school to persuade boys and girls on Thirty-second Street not to use drugs is even more important than anything the district attorney can do to keep drugs off the street. Moving the drug dealers out is important; moving the preachers in is even more important.

"The thing that does not make sense to me," he says, "is for a person to believe that a high school dropout can find supplies of crack and the district attorney can't. We have addicts in our program who were able to find the major drug dealers in Miami and West Palm Beach. And the D.A. can't find these folks? That just doesn't hold water."

Drug abuse isn't just a legal or social problem, it is an economic one. Drugs breed crime and merchants don't want to own stores in areas infested by crime.

"At one point," said Ethel Delaney, "there was not a single grocery store in my entire inner city. Anybody who lived here that did not have access to public transportation, or a car, had to buy food at convenience stores. What they did was jack up prices of things like milk to probably twice what I pay where I shop."

*

The drug problem is nothing new to this country. Sometimes it seems that every five years or so we re-fight a war on drugs, but the scourge never goes away entirely. The reason for this mixed record is clear. The government can do only so much about the drug problem. Without the leadership and involvement of parents, schools, families, church and community leaders, all the government policy and spending won't make a difference.

Occasionally, a few Washington think tanks and professors get together and promote the idea of legalizing drugs. Even our former Surgeon General Joycelyn Elders thought we should study the idea. That may be the worst idea I've ever heard. Although it costs a lot of money to enforce our antidrug laws, the cost of *not* enforcing them would be staggering. Legalization would make drugs easier to obtain and more abundant. What a disaster that policy would be at a time when we are struggling to keep our children away from drugs! William Bennett, who helped steer public attention to the severity of the drug problem when he served as President Bush's "drug czar," called legalization a "moral surrender" in the war on drugs. I agree.

I believe the federal government plays a critical role in enforcing our antidrug laws, especially when it comes to reducing the flow of drugs across our borders. It is virtually impossible for people like Henry and Ethel Delaney to succeed if the streets of Savannah are awash with cocaine and crack. Keeping drugs out of the country is a matter of federal law enforcement and foreign policy. Too many people think we can ignore this aspect of the problem. I don't see how our local drug-prevention efforts can thrive without it.

Of course, those local efforts depend on men like Henry Delaney. There isn't a government program imaginable that can reproduce what he does. If we've learned anything from our decades-long struggle against drugs, it is that there is no better remedy than the character and moral strength of the thousands of local leaders who have been heroic enough to stare down the drug dealers and save countless adults and children from their grasp. We need to learn from Henry Delaney and use his example to inspire others to achieve the same success in their communities. So while there is no shortage of "experts" on national drug policy, it is probably time we started paying attention to the real expertise of men like Reverend Delaney.

The reverend now has sixty preachers affiliated with his church, not all of them ordained, but his goal is to keep buying up the crack houses, moving in his ministers, and pushing out the drug dealers a block at a time, until they're on the other side of the county line.

Before leaving town, I visited with a friend, Savannah's mayor, Susan Weiner. I told her, "You need about fifteen Reverend Delaneys around here."

She threw back her head. "Honey," she said, "if I had fifteen Reverend Delaneys, I wouldn't need nothing."

REUBEN GREENBERG
PHOTOGRAPH BY EARL WARREN

CHAPTER 6

Common Sense About Crime

CHARLESTON, South Carolina

According to its police chief, in Charleston, the crime rate for the last ten years has been 25 percent lower than it was in the decade of the 1960s, even as the city's population grew by 30 percent. That figure covers the three most violent crimes: armed robbery, rape, and murder.

What has happened in Charleston is what I believe can happen around the rest of America. Chief of Police Reuben Greenberg went back in time to "old ideas that still work."

I had been hearing about Reuben Greenberg from Bill Bennett and Jack Kemp, among others, and as we drove out of Savannah, I was eager to meet him. South

Carolina is low country, so flat, if you dropped a marble it might roll for miles. We passed rows of gray mossy trees, and an unusual amount of construction along the highway, a sign of the growing prosperity of such cities as Charleston and Columbia.

We met in a restaurant at the airport and talked over the clatter of dishes and waitresses taking orders. The first thing you notice about Reuben Greenberg is that—in a phrase—he breaks the mold: He is Jewish; he is black; he has been for the past thirteen years the successful chief of a police force based in the deep South.

Reuben Greenberg wasn't in uniform—he wore a tie and a blue blazer—but he exuded authority. He is husky, almost stoic, but his eyes have life and warmth. He had an air of plain talk, common sense, and evangelism, a man of action, not theories. But he has a lighter side. A magazine article I had read about community policing included a photograph of the chief on roller skates.

The city of Charleston is in the midst of a tourist boom, especially in the summer, when visitors fill the hotels to enjoy the lazy charm and southern hospitality. You see them strolling on the streets, transported in time by the gaslights and horse-drawn carriages. The rollback in crime played an important part in this growth, the result, in Reuben Greenberg's words, of attacking "the anonymity that encourages criminals."

What the chief did was go back to the past for the

future. When he was appointed Charleston's chief of police at age fifty, he looked at the ideas that had kept calm and order when he was a boy. He wondered why they were abandoned.

"We used to have something called a truant officer," he said. "In our neighborhood, her name was Miss Cotten. There were others, but she was the one I remember. She drove around the community without a gun, without a car phone or a police radio, looking for kids who had skipped school. She knew all the places we hung out. She would pick us up. She would not present us to any court. She'd bring us back to school. It was that simple. Off the street, back to school."

By the late 1960s, nothing simple survived in the field of education. A different philosophy had taken over, backed by so-called research. The theory was that we wouldn't need truant officers to drag kids to school. The curriculum would be so wonderful, so exciting, so dynamic, so interesting that the janitors would have to step over the students in the morning when they came in to turn on the lights. In the afternoon, the school bus driver would have to lean on his horn to entice them out of the library. The theory didn't work.

Greenberg opened his hands, palms up. "As we sit here speaking," he said, "there are hundreds of police officers all over this country who are stopped at red lights during school hours, watching a kid walk in front of their patrol car—eleven, twelve, thirteen, fourteen, fifteen years old—and wondering why they are not in school. But we never stop and ask them. We expect, somehow, this crime rate for juveniles to just go away, as if by magic."

In Charleston, in 1990, Reuben assigned four cops as truant officers and ordered them to sweep the streets between 8:00 A.M. and 2:30 P.M.—"every kid, tall, short, fat, skinny, black, white, male or female, *before* they snatched a purse, broke into a car or somebody's house. We picked them up and took them back to school. Those who were expelled, we took them home. We removed the option of their being on the street forming gangs. The option was to be in school or in the custody of their parents."

(In Tulsa, when a student skips school, the district attorney threatens to slap the parents in jail. School attendance has gone up.)

In Charleston, when the boredom sank in, the kids started looking for excitement. In the system he inherited, Reuben's cops got awfully good at catching kids in stolen cars. But nothing seemed to happen. No punishment. Not even detention. "We caught one kid five times in one week in stolen cars," he recalled. "The officers said, 'He's only fourteen; what are we going to do to him?' The courts wouldn't take him. There was virtually no punishment for juveniles except for rape or attempted robbery or homicide."

It was not merely a lack of punishment. For juveniles, in many cities, there was no accountability in any meaningful way. Greenberg decided to reinforce the truancy laws because doing so would accomplish two

84

things: It would get the kids out of people's cars, shops, homes, and pocketbooks, and it would reduce their coming together like germs and running in packs.

Just putting four truant officers on the beat caused the daytime crime rate to drop 27 percent in four years. Most school administrators had done nothing because they had no funds for rounding up truants. Their usual policy was to send a letter to the parents if the student missed so many days without an excused absence. The letters had less impact than an advertising flier someone slips under your windshield wiper.

The educators had mixed feelings about the idea of bringing the police into the process. But Charleston was going to try something old. "We are going to get them away from the opportunity to commit crimes," he said, "and put them back in school."

Which they did, and it worked just as it had thirty or forty years ago, in big towns and small, from New York City to Buffalo Breath, Montana, to Maryville, Tennessee.

Having been on the other side—my dad was a school principal, my mother was a teacher, and I have been the president of the University of Tennessee—I wondered how the school principals felt about having all these delinquents returned to the classroom.

The chief grimaced. "To tell you the truth, no one wants to say anything, but their body language tells you they are not happy to see many of these kids. But I make it clear. If they don't want them, expel or suspend them and I will take them home. But as long as they are enrolled as students, they are going to go to school. The state law says so."

Reuben Greenberg doesn't ask for a perfect world. His police force is tested severely in the summer, but he figures he has nine months to clamp down, the kids have three to run loose. He'll settle for that. On practical and legal grounds, he believes his action is correct. In the schools, everything is in place: the buses, the breakfast and lunch programs, the library, the teachers, the tables and chairs. "Everything is there," he says, "except that Johnny wasn't sitting in his chair. We took Johnny from a place where he had anonymity, which makes it possible to commit crimes, and put him in a place where it is much more difficult because the other kids know him."

The truancy program performed so well that the Charleston police instituted another called Operation Midnight. They picked up every kid who could walk under age eighteen, whether they were misbehaving or not, if they were on the street after midnight with no supervision. The parents even "registered" their sons and daughters with the police department. They signed a document listing his or her name with a description, giving police the authority to pick them up and bring them home.

"Kids don't belong on the street at two or three in the morning," said Greenberg. "It's the same thing that everybody did back when you and I were growing up."

One key to the policy was seeing that it applied to all youngsters and all sections of town. There are no exceptions, no favorites, no scapegoats. The result is that in the last four years not a single child that age in the city of Charleston has been the victim of a violent crime, or committed one, during school hours or between midnight amd 3:00 A.M. The reason is that they are not out there, in the places where these acts usually occur.

Let me repeat that fairly startling record: *No person under eighteen years of age has been shot, killed, abducted, molested, or found in the woods in Charleston during those specific hours, in the past four or five years.* To be sure, there are problems between 3:00 A.M. and midnight, when the curfews are not in effect, but the system is not complicated. There is nothing new, nothing punitive about it. Nor do officers find themselves buried in paperwork.

In a town of 100,000, Chief Greenberg has now reduced his staff of four truant officers to two. There are no longer enough truants to keep four cops busy.

I liked what I was hearing, but I was also becoming angry because I was thinking this: Here we are, a country turned upside down by our fear of crime, and the most obvious things to do—we don't do! It takes no Ph.D. to know that young people commit most of the crimes. Especially today, the streets are filled with children who are unloved, unwanted, unattended, uneducated, and who are running around with crack, $3,000 cash, and a handgun in their pockets. We adults are too busy working, and watching TV a record number of hours when we are not working, to become involved.

So we leave it to Congress to pretend to solve the crime problem and throw Congress out when nothing happens.

This is how we get, for example, the Gun Free School Zones Act of 1990, a federal law that bans weapons within one thousand feet of a school. It sounds good. Every single senator voted for it. Now the Supreme Court has said that the law violates the United States Constitution, because Congress has no authority to regulate such local matters. In other words, the Supreme Court has thrown the problem right back into our laps, each neighborhood, each family, each school. Even if we had no Constitution to guide us, I believe the Supreme Court is right simply as a matter of common sense. I can think of two words that will almost never get guns out of schools: federal law. And I can think of two words that will almost always get guns out of schools: personal responsibility.

As U.S. education secretary, I visited a great many schools where there is a zero-tolerance weapons policy that works. It works, not because of some Washington, D.C., law, but because the teachers, students, principals, parents, ministers, rabbis, school board members, and police chiefs all are working together to see that it works.

I carried a pocketknife to school every day when I was growing up in Maryville, Tennessee. Every boy did. But the reason we never even thought about using those knives on each other had nothing to do with the government—it was the families we came from, the nosy neighbors who were so involved in our lives that it was hard to get in trouble, the teachers who taught us right and wrong as well as algebra and English, the churches that were open to keep us busy and out of trouble.

Nothing galls me more than Congress pretending to solve neighborhood crime from Washington, D.C. But I'm equally disturbed by neighborhoods where residents keep their TVs blaring and their schools closed after 3:00 P.M. and then wonder why their streets aren't safe. I can tell you for sure one step that in every community in America would reduce crime, reduce drug use, reduce the number of teenage pregnancies, and increase the academic scores of children. What is this magic formula? Open the schools. Keep them open all year from 6:00 A.M. until the last child wants to go home.

I have visited dozens of schools, from the Bronx to East Los Angeles to Nashville to Miami, that lock their doors at 3:00 P.M. Now, you tell me, in this day and time what sense does this make? In this world of both parents working, of single parents absolutely overwhelmed with their responsibilities, what family schedule operates from 8:00 A.M. to 3:00 P.M.?

Let me give you one example of what can be done—when a community decides to do it. Murfreesboro, Tennessee, a small town south of Nashville that hasn't had a radical thought since the Civil War, has for the last ten years opened its schools from 6:00 A.M. to 6:00 P.M. all year. The extra time is academic, not just day care. The parents pay the bill, fifteen to twenty-five dollars per week. They choose the times their children will attend school. The taxpayers pay nothing. No one poor is turned away. Sixty percent of families use this extra service. This is what I would call Reuben Greenberg common sense. Any community could open its schools in this way, but very few do.

The chief's common sense has made impressive strides against adult crime, too. "If you wanted to get five hundred criminals off the street real quick," said Greenberg, "what would you do? You'd send them to jail. That's where they wind up, sooner or later. If you can keep them there, then you will reduce your crime rate. Period. We oppose a parole for every burglar, every armed robber, every rapist. Those three crimes only, because those are the ones people care about. You can't go after the drug pushers; there are too many of them. The homicides, most of them are crimes of passion and, contrary to what people think, not likely to be repeated. We do go after them occasionally, as well. There are a lot of burglaries, but not that many burglars. One guy may be responsible for fifty or sixty incidents.

"So we are going to oppose their paroles. We are not just going to write a letter. We get in the car and drive to Mobile, Alabama, to the parole board, look them in the baby blues, and say, 'We don't want this guy coming back to our community. This is what he did in our community.' And we take with us the woman who was raped, the merchant who was pistol-whipped, the person whose home was broken into and who can no longer sleep at night.

"We have been doing this for nine years now and we are ninety-three percent successful at keeping them locked up. Only seven percent get paroled who did those three crimes in our city. The board used to grant early parole to seventy-five percent of them."

Meanwhile, his police department cleaned out the housing projects, working with new guidelines drafted by HUD when Jack Kemp was the secretary. Applicants are now screened, and rejected if they have prior records for any of eleven felonies. ID cards are issued. If a mother on welfare with four kids is caught selling crack, she is evicted, and the next day her apartment is leased to another mom on welfare with four kids, one who doesn't sell crack.

We have tolerated for too long the idea that because people are poor they don't object to sending their children to urine-drenched schools or to living with crime. They don't like it any better than anyone else would. They are simply left with no way to deal with it. In Charleston, Reuben Greenberg is able to boast that "no community in our city is safer than public housing." The projects are as safe as the area around any country club.

Ten years ago, taxis wouldn't pick up a fare in the projects. Now the repairman and the pizza delivery van are not afraid to make calls.

Out of one thousand break-ins recorded in Charleston during the last year, less than thirty happened in all the city's public-housing units. Of the eight hundred people arrested for narcotics, ten were caught dealing in the projects. How could this be? The police simply decided to go after the front end. The city decided to become a responsible landlord. Housing officials required the applicants to be employed. They turned down anyone with a felony conviction in the last ten years.

"Just because it's public housing," said Reuben, "doesn't mean you have to take the first yo-yo that comes in." His eyes swept the restaurant around us. "This place would turn into a hellhole real fast if you had armed robbers, burglars, drug dealers coming in and hanging around and doing whatever they wanted to do. What woman would want to go to work, leaving her kids in the yard, with a convicted pedophile living next door and nothing but a piece of sheetrock separating his apartment from hers?"

The housing officials did not implement the screening thoughtlessly. Those who were already living in the units were given a "grandfather" exemption; they could stay as long as they had no recent unsavory record. This eliminated the problem of a mass exodus. Then they controlled the gate, using the permission Jack Kemp gave them to keep out undesirables.

You don't get to be the police chief of a town like Charleston without being streetwise. When a woman is evicted from the projects for cause, the police do it late on a Friday afternoon when, as Reuben puts it, "all the yuppie defense lawyers are at happy hour." The Housing Authority repaints the apartment and cleans it in one day, and on Sunday another woman with children moves in. "On Monday morning, it's a fait accompli. No judge is going to put a woman out of the unit who doesn't sell cocaine, to let one back in who does."

I had to move on and Reuben had a seminar to attend. There was time for one last question. I asked him what could be done about kids who carry guns?

Gently, he reworded my question: "What you need to ask is, why do the kids have guns? They do it for prestige, to show the other kids, not for protection. You don't need a gun to go to school anywhere in this country. The reason they have them is, it's a big macho-type thing. In our state, we have turned it around in a five-county area. We pay them one hundred dollars, not to bring in a gun but to report somebody who has a gun. If we pick up the kid and get the weapon, they get the hundred. We pay them the same day, cash on the barrel head.

"You know what happens now? The kids brag in school that they have a Browning, a Glock, a Magnum. And a fourth kid takes it in and says to himself, 'That looks like three hundred bucks to me.' Our approach is, we are not going to pay for an old gun that has been in the attic since Uncle Jesse died twenty years ago. We are going to get the guns that are active. When a kid boasts that he has a gun, somebody is going to drop a dime and we are going to get that gun."

Reuben Greenberg's smooth and unlined face does not reveal very much, but he looked pleased with his report. I know I was. "You try these ideas over a period of time," he said, "and many of them aren't new, and you find they can make a difference. A big difference."

GAIL, CASEY AND LARRY JOYCE
PHOTOGRAPH BY DEANNA JOYCE

CHAPTER 7

In War or Peace

CHICAGO, Illinois

I had been reluctant to see Larry Joyce. He had sent word that he wanted to see me because, on October 3, 1993, his son Casey had been killed in Somalia. And Larry Joyce, who had himself served two tours of duty in Vietnam, wanted to make sure that anyone who had even the slightest possibility of becoming commander in chief of the U.S. Armed Forces knew the lessons of both Somalia and Vietnam and that many of the lessons were the same.

I suppose that my reluctance to meet with Larry Joyce was because I expected to find him bitter, so bitter that there would not be much to learn from him about policy and, at this point, not much that I could do to ease his grief.

It was late afternoon in Chicago when we met in a small private room in a club in the Wrigley Building. The date was August 17, 1994, two days after he had paid a visit to Arlington National Cemetery to observe the twenty-fifth birthday of his youngest son. "I'm sorry about Casey," I told him. "He would be about the age of my son Drew."

Larry Joyce, I quickly realized, was about my age. His face was weathered and pleasant. His hair was dark, going gray. He has the manner of a corporate executive, and in fact he is one—president for publishing with the American Medical Association. He talked earnestly and quietly, with a contained sort of evangelism. Almost instantly I was glad I had stopped and I listened carefully.

Larry Joyce graduated from Hardin Simmons College in Abilene, Texas, fifteen miles from his hometown of Merkel. He went into the army right out of ROTC. He was an early arrival in Vietnam in 1963 as an adviser to a Vietnamese infantry battalion. He rotated home, spent two years there, and went back in '67 to fly choppers. After his military duty he went to work for Ross Perot's Electronic Data Systems.

His name became increasingly familiar to Americans during July and August 1994. His letters and articles were appearing on the editorial pages of major newspapers, including *USA Today* and *The Wall Street Journal*. He was hammering away at the mistakes he believed had been made in Somalia, and a personal audience with President Clinton had only intensified his efforts.

His son Casey was twenty-four when he died, about the age his father had been when he went to Vietnam on his first tour. He was one of eighteen members of the 3rd Ranger Battalion to die in Mogadishu, in a clash with militia controlled by the clan leader, Mohammed Farah Aidid. I remembered seeing photographs of Rangers who had been killed. They were handsome and wholesome-looking, young men who would have made proud any parent who had raised children, tried to teach them values, hoped for them, feared for them, and felt pride in their every movement.

I wanted to know more about James Casey Joyce. He was the third of three children born in the 1960s, in Dallas. He spent three years at the University of Texas and what was then North Texas State. Then one day he came home and told his father, "I don't know what I want to do with my life. I'm wasting my time and your money. I think I'm going to join the army."

Larry Joyce applauded that idea. "I thought it would mature him," he said. "I've never seen a person come out of the army unchanged. In most cases they have improved. Some go the other way, but they all change. I assumed he was going in for two years and learn a skill. He said, 'No, I'm going into the Rangers.' That was a four-year commitment. I asked him if he had any idea what the demands would be. He said he did. I think he wanted to prove to himself that he could take the toughest assignment the army could offer, and do it well. And he did."

Engaged when he went into the army, Casey married DeAnna after he finished basic training. His father recalled how he would bring his field manuals home at night and study them. "I told my wife," he said, "that I had never had troops like that. I really felt that way. I thought I had never seen a soldier quite like him . . . until I went to Fort Benning and I saw a whole battalion of them. That's what they have today, the kind of young people who are willing to make an extraordinary commitment. That is why I think it is so vital that the commander in chief understand the very precious resource that he has at his fingertips."

Casey was among those who died under heavy fire while trying to rescue the wounded and recover the bodies of the crewmen who had been killed when a helicopter was shot down. "Those young men," said Joyce, "live by a code that I don't think Bill Clinton understands. Matter of fact, maybe a lot of us don't understand it. Can you imagine a code that says, regardless of the circumstances, I will not allow one of my comrades to fall into the hands of the enemy, whether he is dead or alive? That's what happened. No one had to give an order to go secure the helicopter. When it went down, they came running."

When Casey was killed, Larry turned his grief into action. He immediately started asking questions about the events before and after his son's death. "There were several things that just didn't ring true," he said. On his own, he conducted an informal, but fairly thorough, investigation of what had taken place in that neighborhood of shadowy alleys in Mogadishu. He drew his own conclusions about what had gone wrong from a tactical standpoint. "I decided there was something terribly wrong with the mission in Somalia," he said, "not just the strike that was launched on October third, but the entire rationale that led us to change the policy from one of humanitarian relief to one of direct combat."

I asked him if he meant the original concept of the mission, and he said no, just the fact that the objective changed in April 1993. "The more I looked at it," he said, "the more parallels I saw between American policy in Somalia and American policy in Vietnam, which may sound like a leap of logic, but not to me."

And so he began to pound out essays on his computer. His first piece appeared in *USA Today* and then the producers for the Larry King show called. He wrote a letter to the president and had it personally delivered on October 22: "I didn't want it to get lost with the eleven thousand other letters that come in every day," he said.

To his credit, the president telephoned the former army lieutenant colonel on November 10. "You could tell he was moved by the letter," said Larry. "I mean, it was the kind of letter you could not just ignore. Basically, what I wrote was that I supported this president, voted for him. Like a lot of people, I thought that there needed to be changes, and the country needed a domestic focus, which we didn't have from the Bush administration.

"But then I was struck, I told him in the letter, by the similarity between the misguided policies of Presidents Johnson and Kennedy and his recent statements about Somalia, Bosnia, and Haiti. . . . Based on my scrutiny of the situation in Somalia, plus what I knew about the morale of the armed forces, I wanted to meet with him. I said, 'You need to hear these things. . . . Your domestic advisers won't tell you. Your foreign policy advisers won't tell you. The people who wear the uniform, who see you on a daily basis, can't tell you. So who else is there if not someone like me?'"

He was in Texas, his home state, when Clinton called, and they talked for fifteen minutes. The president said he wanted to meet with him and they agreed that the next week would be fine. He said someone from the White House would schedule the meeting.

As too often happens in government, after a brief flurry of interest in Larry Joyce, the White House swung into inertia. The week came and went. He called. No one had a clue who he was or why he was supposed to visit. Frustrated, Larry wrote more articles for more papers. In December, on a business trip to New Orleans, he picked up a copy of *USA Today* and read that U.S. troops had been assigned to escort Mohammed Aidid from his headquarters to the Mogadishu airport. He was to be ferried from there aboard a U.S. military transport to Addis Ababa, in Ethiopia, for a peace conference among Somalia's warring clan leaders.

"I was incensed when I read that," he said, spitting out the words. "I immediately sat down and wrote another piece."

Joyce kept cranking out the articles, including one that appeared in *Newsweek*. In May he testified before the Senate Armed Services Committee and just before that he met, at last, with the president and his top security advisers—for forty-five minutes.

"I started off," Larry said, "by telling him I thought the first thing the Senate committee needed to look at was what led to our decision to change the mission in Somalia, from one of humanitarian aid to military intervention. Who made that decision? Why was it so important to capture Mohammed Farah Aidid? Who made that call? What role did Boutros Boutros-Ghali [the secretary-general of the United Nations] play in that decision?"

At that point, Clinton interrupted him. He said that when he became Commander in Chief, General Colin Powell had advised him, " 'The best thing you can do is let the military make military decisions.' I swore then I would not be like Lyndon Johnson; I wouldn't get up at three o'clock in the morning and call the generals in Vietnam and tell them what they should be doing that day. I wouldn't micro-manage the military."

Larry said the president expressed his displeasure with Boutros-Ghali and had threatened to pull all the

U.S. forces out of the U.N. command. "And I listened to that for about ten minutes. Finally, I said, 'Mr. President, I have a question I just have to ask you. . . . It became clear to me in mid-September that you were working toward a diplomatic solution in Somalia and that you had abandoned the notion of a military solution to the problem there.'

"He kind of acknowledged, yes, I was right. I said, 'I even wrote my son at the end of September that I thought the Rangers would be home in October because it was clear that a military solution wouldn't work. It was weeks later, in fact, that I learned Jimmy Carter had interceded for you and made contact with Aidid and then reported back to you that Aidid was ready to negotiate.' He [Clinton] said, 'Yes, that's right.'

"I said, 'So you're confirming for me that you were working toward a diplomatic solution in mid- to late September. And if that's the case, Mr. President, if you were going to negotiate with Aidid, why did the October third raid take place?' And he looked at me with this blank look on his face and I pursued it. I said, 'If you're going to negotiate with Aidid, why put American lives at risk?' He said, 'You just asked the key question. On October third, when I got the first reports, I turned to Anthony Lake and asked, "Why did they launch that raid?" '

"And here's the point. Regardless of what Bill Clinton said about not micro-managing the military, when you have American troops in combat you have a moral, and I think a constitutional, responsibility to make that your number-one priority. Domestic issues can move to the middle burner or the back burner until the crisis has passed. Now, that doesn't mean the president has got to be on the phone and talking to the generals in Mogadishu. What it does mean, and this is the mistake that was made, is that he has got to be constantly informed about what the military is doing and sure in his own mind that the military action is consistent with his foreign policy. And that wasn't done."

It wasn't hard to connect the dots in the fault line that Larry Joyce had drawn. In December 1992, a month after he lost the election, President Bush ordered twenty-eight thousand American troops to Somalia. With the Marines as a spearhead, their assignment was to discourage the fighting among the warlords and provide safe escort for international shipments of food to the starving masses. This was an expressly humanitarian mission. In May, President Clinton withdrew all but four thousand of the U.S. troops, leaving a small contingent in the capital city of Mogadishu as part of the U.N. peacekeeping forces.

Then the factional warfare started anew, and in August four Americans were killed by a land mine, and in a separate ambush six more were wounded. Faced with a rising casualty toll, and with Aidid's militia growing bolder, the Clinton administration dispatched a four-hundred-man elite strike force to join the hunt for the clan leader.

At that point, the policy signals were decidedly mixed. Major General Thomas M. Montgomery, the

U.S. commander, requested heavy armor and weaponry to pursue Aidid. The request was denied. The administration felt such a show of might would be provocative at a time when diplomatic overtures were being made.

No one, it seemed, had coordinated our foreign policy with the military goals. The U.N. high command sought nothing less than the capture of Aidid and his top officers. "Someone," said Larry Joyce, "should have gotten word to the Special Operations command in Mogadishu to just *turn the switch off*. Don't launch any live raids. We're working toward a diplomatic settlement and we need you guys to back off.' "

I glanced out the window. The sun was setting and the light was playing games on the side of the skyscrapers. Larry Joyce had been talking almost nonstop for more than an hour. It was time for me to drive on to Wisconsin.

"Clearly the first mistake was when the mission shifted from humanitarian to peacekeeping," I said. "But the greatest mistake—and your greatest grief— was that Casey was killed on one day and we got out the next, isn't it?"

"We never should have been there unless we were going to see it through to the end," he said. "Let me put it this way: The military is used to enforce American policy. A lot of discretion has got to be used before we ever employ those troops. I mean, they are a loaded weapon. They go where they are pointed. I told President Clinton this, and I said it in my testimony. Before

106

American troops are ever committed into combat, three questions have to be asked: One, is the mission clear? (In Somalia, the mission shifted.) Two, is it in the U.S. national interest? And three, and perhaps the most critical, are we willing to stay the course? Are we willing to put in the resources to do the job right? Are we willing to accept the casualties and pursue it until we have accomplished the mission?"

I don't know of any high-ranking U.S. military figure who, in retrospect, would have answered yes to all of those three questions, as they applied to Vietnam or the second stage of the Somalia operation. Ask the same questions about Desert Storm, and you would get three thumbs up. This was the heart of Larry Joyce's argument, and his reason for our meeting.

"Before any troops are committed anywhere," he said, "the commander in chief has got to make sure that those questions are answered. If you get a no to one of them, then you really need to think about it. If you get two nos, you will probably make a mistake. If you get three, there is no reason on earth to commit those troops."

DAN BIEDERMAN
PHOTOGRAPH BY EARL WARREN

CHAPTER 8

The Sidewalks of New York

NEW YORK, New York

People who have only heard about New York City, or know it through movies or from television, or by seeing it when they are whisked by taxi from airport to downtown hotel, are usually surprised to learn it has neighborhoods.

I lived in one such neighborhood, Washington Square West in Greenwich Village, when I was a student at the New York University School of Law in the early 1960s. My arrival at law school was my first ever visit to New York City. It was a jarring change for a boy from the Great Smoky Mountains.

I remember that first dinner in the city, sitting alone on Bleecker Street in some Italian restaurant, then staying up most of the night gazing in astonishment from my third-floor window at what was going on in Washington Square. I thought it was the strangest collection of people and activities I had ever seen. I was ready to go home the next day.

I decided to stay, but my sense of security was not helped at all when in contracts class I was called on not just to see how I sounded when I talked (which was what I first suspected was the reason), but to determine whether I had enough sense to talk at all (which is what many New Yorkers doubt about southerners).

I plunged ahead with my studies, and after a while, I began to see Washington Square as a neighborhood and to find within the Village many neighborhoods. I picked up the rhythms of my new neighborhood: breakfast every Saturday morning at The Bagel, a deli so narrow you could barely turn around; McSorley's or the Red Garter on Friday night; the newsstand on Sixth Avenue to buy papers. In fact, in New York, from Carnegie Hill to the Village to Wall Street to Spanish Harlem, there are neighborhoods on top of neighborhoods.

All of these neighborhoods, it seemed to me then, added up to a truly magnificent city. This is not a unanimous conclusion. You love New York City or hate it. I came to love it. The great newspapers, the yellow cabs, the tall buildings, Broadway, the Lady in the Harbor, the wealth and brainpower, the seemingly unlimited number of free activities that anyone could do, even the Yankees. I remember thinking when I was there in the 1960s that in New York City there was so much greatness all crammed into such a small space, rising up so high, that one day Manhattan Island would surely sink under the weight of it all.

★

This past May, I was the commencement speaker at NYU Law School on the occasion of the thirtieth anniversary of my graduation. During those thirty years, the law school has gotten better and living in the city has gotten worse. Over those years the federal government has poured in money. Mayor Giuliani strikes me as just the right medicine, tough enough to turn things around. But I believe it will take more than the federal government, and even more than the mayor, which was why on an especially pleasant warm August afternoon during my drive, I parked the Explorer and walked twenty blocks to the offices of Dan Biederman on East Forty-third, near Grand Central Station. Dan Biederman *knows* it will take more than the government.

I wanted to get an answer to this question: What would New York City be like if it were safe, clean, and the homeless so well served that the streets were relatively free of them at least during the day? Could this be done, and how? I think you would quickly agree that if it could be done, a safe, clean New York City would be instantly regarded as the greatest city in the world.

And let me just say right up front that I went into my meeting with Dan Biederman with a bias. After thirty years of experience in both government and the private sector, I have come to this conclusion: There are *very* few things the government can manage better than the private sector. Someone else said it well: Government can be good at steering things, not running things.

The irony for our country is that we pride ourselves on having the greatest free-enterprise system in the world, we have fought wars to preserve it, we insist that everyone else in the world try it, but we don't always practice what we preach. When it comes to turning over our most difficult challenges to the private sector, we are painfully slow. We may be the last country in the world to take our own best advice. In 1987, when our family lived in Australia, the *socialist* government of New Zealand was privatizing virtually every government function. It is happening almost everywhere—but it is only happening sporadically in the United States.

Still, there are some encouraging stories to tell. In Baltimore, a private company has helped turn urine-stenched inner-city public schools into places now fit for children to learn. Privately managed state prisons are now accepted as cheaper and better run than most state facilities. In New York City, I was about to learn another privatization story. The story is one of New York's and America's best-kept secrets—how a private company has actually helped make some of New York City's streets safer and cleaner.

*

Dan Biederman is in his mid- to late thirties. A few years ago, he saw a niche and filled it with two start-up companies that provide private maintenance, job placement, and security services. He is a Harvard MBA, with an undergraduate degree from Princeton; serious face, dark hair, glasses. His rate of speech would gnarl the fingers of the swiftest court reporter.

You have to brace yourself for his vitality and candor. He does not mince words. "The first thing anyone needs to know," he said, "is that money isn't the only answer [to solving a city's problems]. The funding isn't there. We have to accept the fact that some benign, kindly president isn't coming in and making sure that more money goes into the pipeline."

His company, he said, can do supplemental security work to assist New York City's police officers. They cost up to $70,000, which limits the number of officers that can be put out on the street.

"The city's cost of seventy thousand dollars to a police veteran with benefits is above the market."

Now Biederman was not criticizing New York City cops. He has ridden in cars with big-city cops at night, as I have. He has a sense of what they go through. But he also seemed to understand how city government works. So I listened.

"Fifty thousand people are waiting for sanitation jobs in this city. That probably means that city jobs are above the market cost. A sanitation man or woman can work for twenty years and, at age forty, get half-pay the rest of their lives and go on to something else."

I have to admit I was taken aback. I have for years been fighting to transfer money and decisions from

Washington, D. C., to state and local governments, and if this is what big cities do with the money when it gets here, it doesn't help my argument much. If the cities can't serve the people, who can?

The answer is: The people can, in the private sector. This is what Dan Biederman and his associates have been proving. They argue that there are jobs that civilians in the private sector can do the assist government—not just administrative and clerical jobs, but neighborhood cleanliness and security as well.

It should be said right here what you must have already suspected: Biederman is controversial. Not everyone likes his methods or the money he makes. The media have accused the former homeless he hires of using unnecessary roughness to clear out the present street people from the parks. Some former trainees recently alleged they were instructed to rough up homeless people.

If that were true, it would be terribly wrong. But the theory behind what Biederman has been doing is well worth hearing because it is obviously working where nothing else seemed to.

In short, this is about polishing the Big Apple—and a model program for any city short on funds, long on problems. I asked: "What should the next president do to help?"

Biederman doesn't so much answer your questions as pounce on them: "First, he should encourage cities that are attacking their management problems, including six or seven cities that are run by really smart people: Bret Schundler in Jersey City; Giuliani in New York; Ed Rendell in Philadelphia; Richard Riordan in Los Angeles,, Michael White in Cleveland; Steve Goldsmith in Indianapolis, to some extent Richard Daley in Chicago. The are several others."

The walls of his office are literally covered with charts and graphs, architectural drawings and enlarged maps of the areas where his districts operate. With funding from property owners, his districts spend $20 million a year helping the city stay clean and safe.

He pushed his chair back, walked over to the maps, and pointed. "In these two sections of New York City, two districts in midtown, we are, in effect, providing a large amount of the visible service. When you see a person in uniform, he or she is likely to be a district employee. Policing the streets, sanitation, helping the homeless, removing graffiti, removing stickers from poles, planting flowers, caring for trees—we are doing all of these.

"When Mayor Schundler of Jersey City came to New York, someone told him there was an incredible park he had to see [Bryant Park . . . run by his companies]. We showed him around. He said he couldn't believe this was an urban park. It's not that hard. We just modeled ourselves after the people who really know how to run public spaces like Rockefeller Center.

"We are totally reacting against the way these neighborhoods looked before we came in. But we don't run the infrastructure: the water, the subways, or the schools. We don't haul that trash we collect out to

115

dump on Staten Island. The Sanitation Department does. We just clean small things that offend the senses."

The districts are called the Grand Central Partnership and the 34th Street Partnership. The financing is so simple that even an economist can explain it. Three quarters of their budget comes from assessments of the property owners: among them Metropolitan Life (formerly the Pan Am Building), the Chrysler Building, and the Empire State Building. The buildings occupy fifty million square feet in one district, thirty million in another. The assessment is roughly thirteen cents a square foot. "Few of our members resent paying the thirteen cents," says Dan. "They pay the city as much as eight or ten bucks a foot in real estate taxes.

"The city taxes go to run playgrounds out in Queens, hospitals, subways, and a lot of things that are very important to them. But just as important is the fact that the path to their entrance right here is clean, and that no crimes are being committed around the corner, and there is no graffiti."

In 1980, Biederman was working for a consulting firm, American Management Systems, when his new career sought him out. He was, in his word, "a kid," in his early twenties, not long out of college.

"The Rockefellers hired me to redo Bryant Park," he said. "The New York Public Library needed major restoration work in 1980, and the board went to the Rockefellers for a three-million-dollar grant to fix the deferred maintenance on the building. And it started with David Rockefeller. He actually went and looked the place over. Then he called Andrew Heiskell, who was going to become chairman of the library, and he said, 'You must also take care of that park that surrounds the library.' "

So the matter went to the library board. "When they hired me to do the job," said Dan, "they said, 'We don't know how to do it, but you have to fix the park.' "

At the time, he was the youthful chairman of a local zoning board in Manhattan. "A very contentious form of local government," he said, "which constantly criticized the mayor [Ed Koch] for dealing with business growth at all.

"I was a know-it-all and I was chairman of the board as an unpaid job. I had to deal with Donald Trump and the like—what the zoning requirements were, what kind of bonuses they got for doing more than the code required. I wanted to get into this. I took the park job and then I had to look for ways to supplement my income because review processes delayed the park renovation for ten years."

Listening to Dan was like trying to keep up with the bidding at an auction. My notes looked like chicken scratchings.

"We found that under state laws," he said, "you can establish a business improvement district, or a special services district, very much like a water or sewer district. You have your own source of revenue. The city collects all the money, keeps it for about ten seconds, then relays it to a private nonprofit entity run by someone like me. If an owner doesn't pay, he risks losing his property. Nobody is going to give up the Chrysler Building over an assessment of thirteen cents a foot.

"I co-founded two of these districts in New York City," he went on, adding a touch of wry humor, "with real estate owners who observed that their assets couldn't be moved. They weren't mobile. They had to stay with the buildings they owned. You can't move the Empire State Building to Fairfax, Virginia."

He has boards of directors for the two partnerships consisting of eighty members, mostly the people who own, operate, or occupy the real estate.

Biederman thinks the private sector will eventually manage a big-city school district. "The education community spends more before breakfast," he says, "than the entire electronics industry spends all year. We believe we can manage differently than the public sector. We pick people with good skills, but I am very tough on them. I have real control. I can fire people who don't do the job. We have merit pay. My directors help. I have really smart directors, who crack down on me if I don't do the job. I'm worried about doing a good job.

"[Mayors] get cracked down on if they say the wrong thing about the St. Patrick's Day parade. The public doesn't really view mayors as managers. They see the role as partly symbolic, like being king or queen. I'm hired on a different basis. Am I doing a good job of cleaning this neighborhood? Am I making it attractive for real estate people to rent their space?"

I asked about how his companies keep the streets cleaner and safer, and deal with the homeless.

He started in again: "Let me give you the conventional wisdom versus the truth. Security. Conventional wisdom: 911 is a good thing. True. But 911 is one of the major reasons we have terrible crime in America's cities. Why? Because when 911 was put in, police departments had to respond to all these calls, and our cities are huge. You can't respond on foot. Most 911 calls today are unfounded. You could get a list of every 911 call made in New York last year and just look at, say, page 117. You would be looking at 'Cat in a tree,' and 'Unfounded report of a man with gun.'

"People know by now that if you want to get a cop to your house, you say there is a man with a gun outside. Ninety percent of the time, there isn't any man with a gun. A knife won't do it, see. The report says, 'Report unfounded. Guy with gun no longer there.' All the police can do all day is sit in patrol cars in most American cities and follow up these 911 calls.

"My head of security is a former two-star assistant chief of the New York City Police Department, who had to audition for the job. I asked him what police work is like today. He said, 'We arrive at the scene, find out what has already happened, write reports that are very erudite, take a lot of care in doing our research, fill it out and file the report on the shelf and go on to the next job.' This isn't what we need.

"We need prevention. We don't believe in hiring armed security guards, so we need guys who are in uniform, of some size. We need guys who are intimidating without using guns, who can stop wrongdoers from preying on the rest of us. They ought to be six feet two, two hundred pounds, and fast, if possible, because a guy who arrives at a scene who is six two and weighs two hundred has a much better chance of subduing someone than someone who is five three and weighs one fifty."

People who run for political office hear all kinds of things. But I've seldom heard such blunt candor. If I looked a little uncomfortable, it certainly didn't stop Biederman.

"This is all politically incorrect, of course, because we also need to have women cops and we can't discriminate according to size. But some feel women cops don't do as well in these situations because, generally, they are not as big. We decided we would put guys in uniforms very much like the ones used by the police and have them circulate throughout these districts on routes that were small enough that you would have a definite chance of seeing them.

"And we tell them: 'These are the crimes on post and we want them prevented.' When we started, the level of drug selling up and down Vanderbilt Avenue was horrible. The drug selling in and around Bryant Park was horrible. We removed these bad conditions. How did we do it? We put ourselves in the middle of them: guards with bulletproof vests, unarmed but preventing the conditions by being visible, with a direct radio link to the cops; not through 911 but through their dispatchers. So the response time can be fifteen seconds or it could be two minutes, but it won't be twenty-seven minutes later."

I'm not sure anyone would be willing to place a bet that you could reduce crime in New York City with unarmed patrols. They do it in London. Why not New York?

"Except for the supervisors, who are mostly former NYPD sergeants and have pistol permits, everyone else is unarmed," said Dan. "They just do it by the wisdom of their training and temperament. Our force is almost entirely made up of minorities. No one has ever said to me, 'You have a bunch of racist cops' or 'You're going in and making life miserable for minorities.' Our guards are nearly all members of minority groups themselves. That's the market for security. They might cost half the money an NYPD officer does, but they are extremely well trained."

Without pausing, Biederman moved to the next subject:

"The homeless. There are two conventional wisdoms: One group believes that these are very unlucky people who are in this predicament because of the callousness of our society and the oppressive economic system that put them on the streets. The second group believes that these are crazy people who are just hopeless. They all want to be on the streets. They can't be worked with, and should be treated as criminals.

"Both of these judgments are ridiculous. The truth is, yes, many are troubled, some had a terrible upbringing. Many are mentally ill to some extent. But if you put me out on the street and told me I couldn't go home, to live for a month, I'd be mentally ill by the end of that time. It is a very hard life out there. They are out there for a lot of reasons.

"One is to get away from the system. A lot of them are hiding on the streets. Very few want to be there. A lot of them have drug and alcohol problems. The way to get them off is to give them a better alternative. I would say ninety-five percent of them make rational choices. If you give them a better alternative to being on the street, they will come off the street. We started with food, good meals, far better than the meals they were getting on the streets."

On my drive across the country, I had been in big cities and small, had visited shelters and talked to police chiefs about their solutions to this problem. The cost to society and to human dignity can't be measured. It violates our sense of order; it grates on our conscience; it leaves us brooding about the fate of our cities.

Dan Biederman's partnerships take a different, more positive approach. In a building they lease from the archdiocese, they serve five-course meals to the homeless. Inside a very pleasant dining room, they sit at a table for eight. It is a social environment.

"They eat good meals," he said. "They get to know each other. That was part of the lure—showers, humane treatment, reading material, videos. They are just off the street. The next step is to use peer pressure.

Everybody wants to do better than the next guy. So we issue membership cards. When they hit the first month in our center, we give them a card that says they have reached the blue level. This means they are allowed to get meals and showers at the center.

"Then we separate the blue-card members from the rest, those who have established with us that they want to get out of homelessness. We make a speech the first or second week they are there: All of you who don't want to be on the streets anymore, we will get you jobs and apartments if you want them. Those who raise their hands, we ask to be here at three-fifteen tomorrow. Half the people show up. We tell this group, these are the things we want you to do, and give them another meeting time. We say, we've gotten to know you, we've explained the rules to you, we want you to get to the next level.

"Half of this group drops out. A lot of them have problems that keep them from continuing. But at the door you keep admitting more and more people. You look for those who are truly ready to go into an employment program. Then we put them through a four- to nine-month work-training program, with a stipend, which we call a pathway to employment. The entire philosophy of the program is peer pressure, a desire to be better than the next guy. If they get a job, the other problems will go away. You rarely hear this from the so-called homeless advocates. They say, 'Oh, the mayor doesn't have enough drug placement slots' or 'The feds cut this.' We believe the homeless want something to do. It's not only that it's a job. It's the fact that they need to be somewhere from four P.M. to midnight, or all day on a steady basis.

"When we first set up the program, five years ago, we started out with thirteen people. I walked over to the center and kept track of how it was going. They said, 'It's amazing. Of the thirteen, ten are pretty good workers and of those, four are stars. We're ready to move them into regular employment.'

"To the surprise of those in charge, the homeless would show up early for work—not ten minutes, but often six hours early. When they were asked why, the reply was invariably the same: 'I'm afraid I would miss my chance, I'd screw it up. I'm sleeping in a park in Queens and I was worried I wouldn't make it on time. I wanted to be here so I wouldn't miss my turn.' "

The all-business Dan Biederman was beaming. "We saw that these guys really wanted a chance to get out, and they wanted something to do. They were so proud. They would grab me and say, 'I'm on a green card now and I'm getting to the next level. I'm going to make it. And I want you to raise my salary.' " He laughed, "They always hit me up for salary increases.

"Another interesting twist. We polled the homeless on the streets. The conventional wisdom was, well, they are all out there because of the callousness of our society, of Reagan and Bush and the mayor and governor. We gave the homeless a questionnaire that asked why they were homeless. It contained the one key question, which was, who do you blame for your situation? We gave them a multiple choice: your family, the government, Mayor Koch, your last landlord, your last employer. In the middle of it, buried in there, was 'yourself.'

"They picked it out. Seventy-two percent of them said, I'm responsible. Myself. I'm out here because I screwed up in some way. Turned out to be a list of things, such as stole from an employer, hit my wife, stole from my mother, was hooked on drugs . . ."

I found myself agreeing with Dan Biederman, with his message and his methods, which can best be described as blunt as a shovel. Both his actions and his success say exactly what we as a nation are supposed to believe: that the government should not impose itself where private citizens can serve each other.

If we are to recapture our confidence about our future, to rekindle the promise of American life that tomorrow will be better than today and every one of us can have a part in that better future—then it is essential that experiments like this one in New York City succeed.

The question I wanted to explore was whether big cities are really governable anymore—and how? Could what Dan Biederman is doing in two districts of Manhattan be done all over Manhattan, all over New York City, in other great cities of America? After all, Biederman's successes have occurred in a very small segment of a very large place.

But when you measure progress in people, no number is small. Biederman's program has taken six hundred vagrants off the street and into apartments. He says over two hundred and fifty of them are fully employed and paying their own way.

"One argument," he said, "is that there are no apartments for these people. But if they can have an income of even nine thousand dollars a year, minimum wage, there are market-ready apartments in New York City. We start them in YMCAs. They behave in rooms. When they pass through the YMCA standards, we think we can confidently represent them to a real estate broker as being apartment-ready.

"The other thing is, we know these people, so we look for them on the streets. The six hundred I mentioned, we don't see them anymore. That leads to another conventional wisdom. According to the advocates, there are hundreds of thousands, even millions, of homeless in the country. The truth is, there are far less than the advocates say. Sometimes, people inflate the numbers for their own purposes. In New York City, they argue that there are over a hundred thousand homeless. Our research says there are about ten thousand who are really on the street.

"Look at our districts. We have Penn Station, Grand Central. This is where everybody thinks the homeless are. In our districts, we can count them. The number is now less than twenty-five who don't get fed, don't get a place to sleep, who go unserved. The figure is low because we have persuaded hundreds of them to come into our center and get started toward jobs and apartments."

126

I was curious. Did they ever actually go out and try to count the homeless?

"That's what we did the first night, March thirty-first, 1989, when we did our poll. We counted six hundred and twenty-two people, including children, and that covered Grand Central Station, even the bowels of the terminal. Of those, we think about twenty or thirty of them are still out there today. Some have died. Some may have moved to South Carolina, but the vast majority are off the streets because that is the group we worked on. Some of them are still in our center right now, sitting up in chairs. Unfortunately, some have been there for years.

"It's not a shelter. It's a drop-in center. We tell them, we don't want you sitting in a chair forever. We don't want you to just hang around here. We want you to have a home. We can get you an apartment. Some don't have the aspiration to do it, but a hell of a lot of them do and you can help them. It takes awhile. The best way is to give them something to do."

A dozen or so banks, including Chase Manhattan, Chemical, and Citibank, pay a premium to have the street patrols monitor their automatic teller machines. "We go to the machines," said Dan, "and see if anybody is in the vestibule. If they are, we talk them out of there. NBC News did a show on it. The work is done by guys who used to be homeless, who now make anywhere from ten to thirty thousand. Some of them are really on a management track. We have one married couple who now have a joint income of around forty-four

thousand. They were homeless two years ago. I'm trying to be objective when I say this is the most successful
social service program in New York City.

"It's controversial. The advocacy community doesn't
like us. They don't think businesses should be allowed
to run these programs."

I asked him what his customers expected. If he had
to make a list, what would be the first objective?

"They want Bryant Park," he said, "to be as safe as
the Luxembourg Gardens in Paris. We've done that.
There were one hundred forty-four robberies a year
back in 1979. We haven't had a crime in here since we
reopened it two and a half years ago. We used as our
model all the good urban parks in the world. This is no
secret. You go and look and see what they are doing
that works. Excellent maintenance. No graffiti. Bathrooms better than the ones in Union Station in Washington, D.C. We keep them really clean, with flowers
here and there. Now we schedule concerts, lectures,
plays, readings.

"When you draw people, the security becomes self-
enforcing. We are supplemented by the NYPD, but it's
basically us, our security force in the same kind of uniforms. They walk the park, a staff of fourteen people,
three or four to a shift. They cover nine acres, including
the library. We restored five acres of lawn and beautiful
gardens.

"There is a way to tell if people believe that a facility
is safe. You count the number of men and women who
use it. Rockefeller Center draws fifty percent men and

fifty percent women. That means women haven't made a decision to stay away because of personal security fears. We have great lighting. So even at nighttime, we don't give it back to the bad guys."

I tried to put myself in the role of a property owner. If I supported Dan's districts, what are the first three things I would want achieved? His response:

"In these districts [meaning in the middle of Manhattan] the answer is clearly safety, sanitation, and clearing of the streets. Sanitation is maintenance, graffiti, and trash. The conventional wisdom is, New Yorkers aren't neat, no way you can keep this place clean. Also, there is no money from Washington. The truth: It's very simple. And it isn't high technology. What do we see outside? Brooms, shovels, people in white uniforms emptying cans, sweeping. Inside, we give them a schedule, hire good managers, make sure they enforce the standards, use computers, give merit pay, make sure they work eight hours, don't let them chat.

"If you see something wrong, you go out there. In our district, if you look out on the curbs, our force is through sweeping at seven P.M., so it gets dirty after that. This is mainly an office district. We start the next morning at seven A.M., before the commuters return. It's clean when they arrive, clean when they leave. When they go home, they don't complain anymore about the filthy place they just left. This area, in the downtown blocks, is cleaner now than where they live in the suburbs.

"Everybody told me we couldn't fix these neighborhoods," said Dan Biederman. "Every time we did, they said we couldn't do the next one." But they kept cleaning them up, with a plan that can be applied to the problems of any city in America. The political priority should be to find the people with the skills to get the job done, then get out of their way.

Biederman says: "Let us focus on the substance. No politics. Just make the decision. *You* take the credit and give us the money to do the job."

That formula sounds to me like free enterprise at work.

ROBB RAUH
PHOTOGRAPH BY EARL WARREN

CHAPTER 9

The Desk in the Hall

MILWAUKEE, Wisconsin

"Nobody's children should be compelled to attend a
bad public school."

—Diane Ravitch

It wasn't hard to find the principal of the Urban Day
School. His desk was smack in the middle of the main
hallway.

The location of Robb Rauh's desk was only the first
indication I had that this was a different kind of school.
It sat in front of a blackboard festooned with notes and
schedules and drawings. Robb's chair is in *front* of the
desk, facing two others, closing the space between the

principal and the students who have a need to meet with him.

One of the parents in the room when I arrived, Alma Walton, worked with a lady named Polly Williams, who circulated petitions and lobbied her fellow state legislators until they agreed to offer poor families an alternative to the public schools.

I had driven to Milwaukee specifically to get a firsthand look at how its school-choice program was working. As a governor, university president, and education secretary, I have seen that nothing is more important to our future than a first-class education system available to everyone, especially poor families. It is the surest ticket from the back to the front of the line.

But I have also seen what deep ruts our schools are in, and how hard it is to make real changes. For ten years I have been persuaded that giving parents the choice of the schools their children attend will create the maximum opportunity for children and the best schools among which they may choose. Incredibly, the only program in America in which public funds are used to give poor parents an opportunity to choose among public and private schools is in Milwaukee—and it is limited to one thousand children. It was enacted after courageous efforts by Representative Polly Williams and Governor Tommy Thompson. I had followed the program closely and wanted to catch up on how it was working.

Alma Walton's daughter Kayla was a first grader

when Urban Day School began accepting vouchers in
1989. She had four other children who had been students there, paying a tuition offset partly by her hours
of volunteer work for the school. "It was a sacrifice for
us to have the kids in here, on my husband's salary,"
she said, "because at the time I wasn't working. I
started with my son Wayman, who was in the public
schools up to the fifth grade.

"I didn't feel he was getting what he needed. The
classes were larger. When I met with his teachers, they
didn't have enough time to sit down and explain what
he was going through, or how I could help him at
home. He was beginning to get discouraged, didn't care
if he made high grades or not. When I went and sat in
on the classes, they were so disruptive. The teacher
wouldn't stop a class and get the kids back in order. If
they got it, fine. If they didn't, she had to continue the
lesson. It's different here. The class size is small. The
teachers are willing to spend more time with the kids.
I felt that from my oldest child to this one. If Kayla
needs extra help, the teachers will call right away."

She wasn't blaming the public school teachers because the classes are too crowded, or the system is too
big, or the buildings are no longer safe. But these were
the reasons she joined with Polly Williams to fight for
another choice.

Urban Day goes through the eighth grade, with an
enrollment of just over three hundred students—two
hundred of them now in the choice program. They

wear uniforms, no designer labels on their clothes, no risk they will be robbed of their name-brand tennis shoes.

"I feel secure here with my kids," she said. "Since the school is so much smaller, I don't have to worry about gang-related problems. I don't have to worry about drug-related problems or teen pregnancy. They are more sheltered in a smaller school. They are getting a sense of self-worth. And when they leave here, if they choose to go to a public high school they will know they can function."

The parents get involved in the school in a direct and meaningful way. If they miss an all-parent conference, they can make it up by going to school and watching a video. If they miss the video, the student is suspended for a day or the parent has to pay a ten-dollar fine. The money adds up; so does the embarrassment. The parents sit on the board of directors. They work on committees.

Mr. Higgins enrolled his daughter, Chironda, a fifth grader, after the homeowners voted down a bond issue for the Milwaukee public school system. "They said they needed money to repair the buildings," he said, "for books and supplies. I more or less got tired of the politics of the public school system. I'm not blaming it all on them. I know that a lot of it starts at home. But I felt my daughter would receive a better opportunity here to prepare herself to go to high school, and beyond. We all know that without college, she's walking a dead-end street."

Chironda wasn't exactly thrilled with the move. The students at Urban Day have fewer holidays, more homework, and longer hours—1,100 hours of instruction compared to 875 as a public school average.

"It was an adjustment for her," said Mr. Higgins. "But before I enrolled her, I came up here and talked to the people and I knew what she was getting into. It brought joy to my heart because I know it will pay off for her. It was my decision and she has to live with it. But down the road, she will be happy that this decision was made for her."

This is how the Milwaukee program works: It is limited to one thousand eligible children, and to 65 percent of a private school's student body. The voucher issued by the state is worth $2,970 and pays the full tuition. In-kind donations—such as volunteer work—cover the other costs related to a child's education. I asked Robb Rauh, "So the parents don't have to pay anything out of pocket?"

"Not unless they miss the meetings," he said. Everyone laughed.

I asked Mr. Higgins if he would be able to send Chironda without the voucher. "For me," he said, "it would be almost impossible. I worked as a machinist for twelve years. I have disabling back injuries, so I'm going back to school myself, to Milwaukee Area Technical College."

Added Mrs. Walton: "It was a struggle for us. We had to give up some things, such as eating out. We knew this was something we wanted for our kids. With the

137

other kids, it helped that you could put in so much volunteer time and that came off your tuition."

An independent school, with no church affiliation, Urban Day has a waiting list of fifty students. It spends about $3,000 per child, roughly half what the Milwaukee public schools spend.

"We have seen some miraculous turnarounds," said Robb Rauh. "There is a real sense of accountability. We have one kid who graduated from the eighth grade, who comes every day just to help out. We hired him for part of the summer as a youth worker, but even though his job is over, he's still hanging around. He was not a good student when he came here, but because the teachers stayed on his back and kept encouraging him, he will be an asset to whatever high school he attends. He has learned to be responsible.

"We had one kid I started working with in the seventh grade, who didn't do any homework. He was in la-la-land. He just struggled and floundered the whole year. We kept after him, kept after him. He repeated the seventh grade. He graduated this year with a solid B average. He was captain of the basketball team and organized several dances and fund-raising events. He will be very successful in high school. Before that, he was slipping through the cracks."

Alma Walton described that first bus trip she made with other parents to the state legislature in Madison, to lobby for the school-choice program. "We watched and listened," she said, "and when some of us tried to voice our concerns we were told to shut up or leave. They didn't let us say anything."

I asked her if there was more support now, or if the program is still under attack?

"I don't hear much about anyone attacking it anymore," she said. "I think the word is out there and people see it works. The only time you hear something negative is when it comes from the teachers' union."

"Most of the time," added Mr. Higgins, "you know the union will be against it. But Howard Fuller [who recently resigned as the head of the Milwaukee public school system] has been trying to get the city to approve the hiring of nonunion teachers. So that, in itself, is a pat on the back for this program. They can't ignore the problems in the public schools. They showed a film clip on the television news of a school where the kids were gambling, sitting on the desks, partying, and having a good time. The teacher had his feet up, reading a newspaper.

"I've had to come here sometimes to pick up my child and I don't see any kids walking the halls. They treat me with respect. They know I am Chironda's father. They call me Mr. Higgins. They say 'sir' and 'ma'am.'"

School choice won't make all the ills disappear overnight. The guns won't turn to chalk, the test scores won't soar, and not every student will be motivated. But one parent compared it to "the law of the farm." Meaning, you plow the ground, plant the seed, and in due time, if all goes well you harvest the crop.

"According to the test results," said Robb Rauh, "our kids aren't doing any better than the kids in the public schools. That is probably the biggest point the critics have lobbed at us. But test scores are not the only indicator. Among the things we look at is parental satisfaction. Overwhelmingly, the parents are satisfied with the experience their kids are having. They feel their children are safe here. One mother sent her kid here after someone pulled a gun on him in a public school. They value that safer environment.

"We do have some turnover from year to year, seventeen percent. But that's not unusual for an urban school. We are doing well enough that there is talk that the program might be expanded statewide. I think that would be great, but it also makes me a little nervous. Right now we are kind of in this wonderful little nirvana, small enough that the teachers' union and the political interest groups have left us alone.

"Even the Department of Education has been very hands-off. We have to file certain things and follow certain guidelines. But they haven't imposed a lot of regulations on us. They check to make sure we are doing what we say we are doing."

As I sat there listening, taking an occasional note, I must admit I was not very objective. I want the voucher program to work because I believe it will benefit our public schools, not diminish them. People need choices. Diane Ravitch said it best: "Nobody's children should be compelled to attend a bad public school."

"I don't look at it," said Rauh, "as something that will

hurt public education. I look at it as being a competition, which I think is healthy. The way the program is set up right now, the public schools actually have more money to spend on their remaining students. We get the state money; they still keep the city money that they would have spent on these additional thousand kids."

I raised some of the criticisms I always hear: Are you taking the best students from them? Are you skimming off the cream?

"People say that," Robb replied. "I mean, that is one of the charges, that we get the cream of the crop. But anyone who comes in here and really looks at the program will attest that this isn't true. They also say the opposite: These are low-income parents, meaning that they don't know enough or care enough to see it through. Look around the room. As you can see, these are pretty typical parents. They know exactly what is going on and they care an awful lot about what is happening to their kids.

"Here the parents finally feel as if they are in control of something. And that carries over to the kids. They feel they have a voice in their own destiny. They can make choices that will affect what they are going to do with their lives."

*

I am always angered by the assumption that anyone who is poor is also dumb and uncaring. It suggests that people who happen to be poor are happy to live in dangerous housing projects and send their kids to urine-stenched schools. The truth is, poor parents have more, not less, incentive to help their children out of poverty. Not all will. But that's no reason to consign poor children to the worst schools.

Most parents want what is best for their children. President Clinton's late mother drove him every day into Hot Springs to go to a good Catholic school because she wanted the best for him. My grandfather sold his farm and moved to Maryville because he wanted my father and his brothers and sisters to attend better public schools. There was such a difference that "your father thought he had died and gone to heaven when he enrolled in Maryville High School," my mother told me.

Yet in a nation of 55 million children, only 1,000 in Milwaukee have enjoyed the privilege of using government money to choose among the best schools in town—and even that money could be spent at religious schools. (The good news is that the Wisconsin state legislature recently expanded the school choice program to include 15,000 students.)

Let's be clear about what is at stake here: our entire future. Everywhere I went on my drive, most of those with whom I talked saw a growing number of Americans who were becoming stuck at the back of the line. Our country will explode if that continues. It violates the promise of American life—that every single person will have an opportunity to participate in the unlimited future that we have always believed is out there for Americans who work hard.

Most people also agree on what it takes to help someone move from the back to the front of the line. First, a job, some prospect of economic opportunity. Second, a family that nurtures and creates the character and values it takes to hold and succeed in that job and in life generally. Third, the opportunity to go to a good school.

The public education system we have in America today takes the very students who most need to attend the best schools and freezes them into the worst schools. Think about this: If you have money, you move to a neighborhood with good schools. Or you put together enough for private-school tuition. If you have no money, you and your child are stuck.

I must warn you, this is probably the most controversial idea in American public education. The unions and most public school officials are dead-set against it. This can be overwhelming opposition. I found that out in Tennessee in 1983 and 1984 when I fought for a year and a half to pay our teachers more for teaching well. For as long as I was governor, I had to threaten to veto teachers' pay raises, and I actually did it once, in order to force a compensation system that included some pay-for-performance.

We won the fight, but unfortunately we are still the only state to pay teachers more for teaching well. And Milwaukee is still the only city to use public money to allow poor parents to have choices of public and private schools. (Although a small choice program is starting in Cleveland.)

I am nevertheless optimistic about the future. I believe resistance to school choice is the Berlin Wall of domestic policy issues. One sunny day the opposition to it will crumble and everyone will ask: How, in America, did we support for so long a system that gave everyone except the poorest families an opportunity to choose the best schools for their children?

After all, this is hardly a new idea in America. After World War II, the government gave scholarships to returning veterans, who spent them at the colleges of their choice. No one said, "You can't go to Notre Dame, or Yeshiva." Not only did the sky not fall, the government money and the competition for students helped create expanded opportunities and the best system of higher education in the world. What the GI Bill did for veterans and higher education, a GI Bill for kids could do for elementary and high school students—and their schools.

I can think of nothing that would make more difference in helping our country recapture its confidence than turning our system of elementary and public education upside down and giving parents, teachers, and communities a chance to start over.

As I look into the future, here is what I see: Schools open until late in the evening, six days a week all year. Parents choosing the schools and the school hours they believe are best for their families. Many more different kinds of schools springing up, at locations convenient for working families, with curricula that meet the needs of children of many different backgrounds. For example: schools that immerse English-speaking children in French; schools for eleventh and twelfth graders who are not going directly to college but want to get a job as soon as they graduate; schools located in corporations or universities or libraries or zoos; schools that emphasize math or science or language or the arts.

I would expect to see an increase in home schooling—but home schooling tied more closely to the options available in the public schools. Master teachers would be paid $80,000 per year; some teaching contracts would be year-round. Teaching would be so attractive professionally that there would be long lines waiting to be employed. This would all be "public education," since government money would be used, but it would be a very new definition of public education.

How do we get there? These simple steps:

First, we should move all decision making and money for elementary and secondary education out of Washington, D.C., and put it back in the hands of parents and teachers who are closest to the child. This means abolishing the U.S. Department of Education.

Second, states and cities should give all the money they spend on elementary and secondary education to parents and let them spend the money at the school or schools that offer the educational programs that the parents believe are best for their children.

Third, the nation's fifteen thousand school boards

145

should forget about managing schools themselves. Instead, they should invite the most creative people in their communities to come up with the best proposals to help children learn. This would include private and religious schools. The school board's job would then be to make sure that those schools are safe and sensible, and that children are learning. As long as parents choose from among these schools the best school for their child, government money should follow the child to the school.

Should there be a federal law requiring this? Absolutely not. Parents and communities must create their own school systems. Can a president of the United States committed to such a vision of American public education help it happen? Absolutely yes. I learned when I was governor that a chief executive who throws himself into something important, with everything he has, for as long as he is there, can usually wear everyone else out. If I were the president, I would do that to advance this picture of America's future in education.

These three steps would by themselves create a revolution in American education that would make our elementary and secondary schools as good as our colleges and universities. And most important, nobody's child would be made to go to a bad public school. That, to me, is an essential part of the promise of American life.

146

HENRY RONQUILLO

EVELYN AND ROLLIE BALANZA
PHOTOGRAPHS BY EARL WARREN

CHAPTER 10

We Are All Americans

LOS ANGELES, California

Driving west is the way to experience America. Especially from Grand Junction Colorado, toward Los Angeles, the horizon, like our country, seems to be an unlimited opportunity: power lines stringing until you cannot see them, the interstate itself a narrowing gray into the brown distance, fences and long lines of trucks disappearing into the darkness.

I was looking forward to arriving in Los Angeles and seeing Henry Ronquillo again. I especially wanted to ask him about one student who, when I visited Roosevelt High School in East Los Angeles two years earlier, seemed to have such an unlimited opportunity. Henry is the principal of Roosevelt, which has 4,500

149

students, almost all Mexican-American. I was embarrassed to discover that he and his wife had canceled their Labor Day vacation to welcome me. But I quickly asked him about the student he had mentioned when I visited as education secretary.

"You mean Efraim," he said. "He received a community scholarship to Cal State, is majoring in engineering, and worked on the Solar Eagle Project, a contest among universities to design a more fuel-efficient car. He is doing well."

I had never met Efraim but I had thought about him often because I had tried to find private scholarship aid for him two years before. He had straight As and was the class valedictorian in that 4,500-student high school. He had wanted to go to Harvard but was ineligible for federal scholarship and loan programs. The reason: He was in this country illegally.

While I was unpacking, Henry Ronquillo told me about Efraim's younger brother.

"His name is Edain. He was in eighth grade last year. Just as good a student as Efraim," said Henry. "Always does his homework. Making straight As. But last summer the family was out for a Saturday in the community park between Roosevelt High and Hollenbeck Middle School. It was a nice day. It is a nice park— palm trees, tennis courts, flowers, neatly kept. The park was full of people and the boys were playing tennis while their parents got together a meal. Someone drove by and shot into the park. One of the bullets went into

150

Edain's left temple, destroying his left eye and lodging in the temple over his right eye.

"Edain was enrolled at that time in our summer school, taking two academic courses. On Monday, two days later, his father—who speaks no English at all—showed up at the school to pick up Edain's homework. The boy was concerned about his straight-A average and his perfect attendance record. Of course, he couldn't see at all, so the teachers taped his homework for him. We assured him that his absence wouldn't count against his attendance record."

I stopped unpacking the Explorer and sat down on the porch.

"What has happened to him?" I asked Henry.

"He gradually recovered. He came back to school in the fall with the bullet still in his right temple. The sight in his left eye was gone. The vision in his right eye was blurred. He had headaches. I kept asking him when the doctor was going to take the bullet out. And he kept saying he was looking for a doctor who would take the bullet out over the weekend so he would not miss any school!

"Finally he was persuaded to have the bullet removed. We told him we would tape his homework again and give him credit for perfect attendance. The kids in the school and the staff collected thirty-five hundred dollars to help pay for the operation. His father took a nighttime job at the parking lot, making a few dollars an hour."

"Where is he today?" I asked.

"Well, he spent a year with us at Roosevelt and today he is a student at Phillips Andover in New Hampshire. The vision in his right eye is close to normal, but he still has occasional headaches.

"You know, I have kids who sneeze and don't want to go to school, and then I have these boys."

"Did they ever catch the shooters?"

"No," said Henry.

*

The teachers will privately tell you, although no one knows for sure, that perhaps one third of the 4,500 students at Roosevelt are children of families here illegally, and therefore the students are here illegally, too. This violates the law, burdens school budgets, burdens the budgets of all social services, and breeds enormous resentment among families—including recent immigrants—who are here legally.

This phenomenon of illegal immigration led to Proposition 187, in which Californians—a few months after I visited the Ronquillos—voted to cut off education and health benefits to undocumented aliens.

If I had lived in California, I would have voted for Proposition 187. I would have done it primarily to send a message to Washington. There is a right-and-wrong issue at stake here. It is wrong to require some people to follow the rules of admission to citizenship and not require others. It is wrong to collect taxes from those who follow the rules in order to pay the bills of those who don't. And it is wrong for the federal government to dump onto California and other border states the consequences of its failure to secure our borders.

But the stories of Efraim and Edain remind us that for the most part, immigration has been a national asset for our country, not a national liability. There are few stories as touching as Efraim's father showing up on Monday to get the boy's homework after he had been shot on Saturday. But almost all of us can think of families newly arrived in America who have become an inspiration to the rest of us. I remember the Laotian sixth grader who won the Chattanooga spelling bee three years after arriving here not knowing one word of English. Sometimes those who have come here most recently are the best teachers for the rest of us as to what it means to be an American.

That is why I think we should drop the idea of other statewide Proposition 187s—especially a national 187. Instead of focusing on those already here illegally, it would serve us better to correct the situation that permits them to come in illegally in the first place. A country that can put a man on the moon and shoot rockets around corners of buildings should be able to control its borders. A national 187 debate would only arouse anti-immigrant feelings, some of which would be aimed at those immigrants who came here legally. It would make it harder for us to say four of the most important words in the English language: We Are All Americans.

I would even suggest—since California's 187 is still

tied up in court—a different approach that might be legislated in that state: Allow any child who was enrolled in school last year to continue, no questions asked, as long as attendance is above 90 percent and the child is making progress toward a diploma. But to families not yet here, fair warning should go out that they will be sent back, expelled, along with their children, when the new law takes effect. There simply must be that distinction between those who are here legally and those who are not.

*

Henry Ronquillo was born in El Paso, Texas, on the Mexican border, the youngest of seven children. His father moved to California in 1931 or '32, in search of a job, and when he found one at the shipyards he sent for his family. They moved into one of the country's first public housing projects, apartments with a common bathroom for each floor.

This was in East Los Angeles. Henry graduated from Roosevelt High, went to the University of Oregon on a basketball scholarship, and came back to East L.A. Before he was promoted to the principal's job at Roosevelt, he was among a group of teachers who went to Garfield High School in the mid-1970s. Garfield is the other large Mexican-American L.A. high school.

He was there in 1982 when Jaime Escalante prepared eighteen of his students for the Advanced Placement calculus examination and all eighteen made 3 or higher on a scale of 1 to 5. That meant that those eighteen Garfield students represented more than half of all the Hispanic students in America to score that well on that test that year.

The Educational Testing Service concluded that they must have cheated—this was in May 1982—and made them take the test again in August. Despite the delay, despite the attention, despite the monitors, despite the graduation of three students in the meantime, fifteen took the test and again fifteen scored 3 or better.

The story of Escalante and his class was turned into a movie called *Stand and Deliver,* starring Edward James Olmos.

I had breakfast with a group of teachers from the East Los Angeles schools, one of whom was a young woman named Josie who had been in that group of eighteen at Garfield, with Escalante. Josie won a scholarship to UCLA, dropped out when her mother became ill, then went back to college and finished at Cal State. She paid off the family medical bills and eleven years later is teaching again—fourth-year calculus at Roosevelt High School.

I asked her the question I found myself asking almost everyone with whom I visited on my drive. "What about the future? Looking ahead twenty years, do you believe your children and grandchildren will have more opportunities growing up in this country than you have had?"

"I hope so," Josie said. "The reason I am a teacher is to lay the groundwork for it. If it's our children—I'm sure about my own kids. They will have more opportunity. But I'm afraid I'm not so sure about the children of others."

Many adults in East L.A. do not speak English, and most of the parent-teacher meetings are conducted in Spanish. It is the only language everyone understands. But the kids, almost all of them, want to learn English, and their parents push them to learn.

When Ronquillo returned to Roosevelt in 1983, there were four classes of English as a Second Language (ESL). There was an ESL prom night and ESL class officers. "I did away with that right away," he said. "It was a security blanket. They would never get out of there and into the real world. Now the kids move in and they move on."

I asked Henry what the biggest changes have been since he started teaching thirty-five years ago.

"Basically," he said, "the school systems haven't changed that much, in my opinion. There are a lot of myths about what schools are doing today as compared to the past. But to begin with, there is just more of everything. More kids. More distractions. Drugs. Gang activity. I'm talking now about East L.A. We have always had gangs, always had some drugs, always had a lot of kids, but nothing like the volume we have today. I'm not talking about forty years ago. I mean just in the last ten or eleven years.

"At the same time, you have more kids achieving, more kids graduating. The myth is that they are not. You look at the dropout rates. The research shows that back in the 1940s, the dropout rate was huge, much

156

greater than today. We are seeing a demand for kids to finish high school. What I think has happened is, the schools have improved over the years. More kids are taking the SAT. More kids are going to college. They have more opportunities, and the expectations have gotten so high there is a gap between the performance and what the perceptions are. There is a perception that the schools are really deteriorating, falling apart, and I don't think so."

*

California never disappoints you; you can see it changing before your eyes. Once, everything seemed to start in New York and move west. Now California exports the ideas, the trends, even the problems, across America.

As I listened to Henry Ronquillo, it struck me again how much schools struggle with the world outside their own walls.

He nodded. "Yes, that has changed. I remember when I was a tenth grader and a friend borrowed his father's car, so we ditched school. You know, we were cruising. We went to a neighboring high school. We drove to a park and then downtown. We were bored. We ended up going back to school. There were no malls like there are now, no Nintendo games, no place to go check out the girls. Today you can hang out in the arcades. If you have cable TV at home, you can surf through the different channels.

"Of course, when we were kids a parent was usually

157

at home, so you couldn't go home. Today the kids stay at home or sneak back and the parents don't even know because they work, or they are a one-parent family. So we have a lot of distractions competing for the kid's time. When a school brings in its technology, and you are showing some audiovisual things, they are bored because they can go home and watch a million-dollar production on Disney or the Discovery Channel."

Most of the news about immigration seems to originate in California, but the story of immigration and the American dream is a story that is told in almost every neighborhood in this country.

Earlier in my drive, I had stopped in Fair Lawn, New Jersey, and spent the night at the home of a Filipino couple, Evelyn and Rollie Balanza. In 1973 Evelyn came from Manila to Georgia. Seventeen hundred young Filipina girls had been interviewed; thirteen were offered jobs as nurses. She received her citizenship in 1983. Rollie arrived in America in 1979. He received his citizenship in 1984. They have lived in Fair Lawn since 1982." Evelyn works from 11:00 P.M. to 7:00 A.M. at Barnett Memorial Hospital. Rollie is an accountant for an electronics firm that is deeply involved in health care.

Fair Lawn is a town with a large Jewish community and five synagogues. The Italian-American population is the next largest. Then come the Asians, most of them from the Philippines and India.

It was getting toward the end of the sticky summer. I had tried to maintain my habit of taking a long walk each morning during the trip, and felt I had been rewarded when I noticed a loosening in the waist of my khaki pants. But they seemed to be filling up again after the Filipino feast the Balanzas prepared for us: shrimp, *pasnit* noodles, vegetables, sweet and sour perch, beef steak marinated with soy sauce and lemon, rice, and a choice of desserts—*bibingka* (banana leaves), *yuka* flan (a sort of sweet-potato pie), and blueberry cheesecake.

The mix of people in Fair Lawn is an industrious one. I think to myself, this is the way America probably should look to someone dreaming about coming here. My walk takes me along a street of two-story houses, placed snugly together, with marigolds blooming in the yards and garbage cans set neatly at the curb, waiting to be picked up. Old oak trees spread their leaves.

There are enough signs posted to make it clear that this is a town filled with busy neighborhood committees. I pass the Fair Lawn Recreation Center. Tennis only. Members only. No parking. No dogs allowed.

"Personally," Rollie Balanza said at breakfast, "I think I will always feel a little more Filipino than anything else. Perhaps this is because I was in my mid-forties when I came here. That isn't to say I'm not proud to be an American. It's just that my cultural ways had been shaped for forty-five years."

I mentioned that a friend of mine in Miami, a Cuban American, says there is a distinct difference between the attitudes of those who came to America at twelve and those who came at twenty.

"Our children have been here since they were five or six," said Balanza. "I think they have more of the feeling of the second generation. You have to understand. We come from a Third World country. In a country as poor as the Philippines, you don't think about being nationalistic. You think about having the money to feed your family. The number-one goal is to educate your children. No matter how poor a family, they will send their children to school so they can get a degree. We come here highly qualified, hoping to be able to express ourselves and to be whatever we are supposed to be.

"We forget about being nationalistic, being political, being this or that. You may not know this"—and I didn't—"but a large percentage of the doctors in New Jersey are Filipinos. The median income of the Asian population in New Jersey is thirty-six thousand dollars a year, much higher than Hispanics and blacks, higher than most whites."

There are about fifty Filipino families in the area, and Rollie and his wife—who is known as Nelzie— were among those who left when Ferdinand Marcos imposed martial law, after the murder of the opposition leader, Benigno Aquino.

"It is a matter of pride," said Rollie, "that you have to amount to something here and you can't go back. We sort of took the last plane out, as far as having the opportunity to come. I didn't really want to leave until the day Aquino was slain."

He has been here a relatively short time. While others debate the issues of immigration and foreign aid, he has lived them. "That is why I'm ambivalent," he said. "I would like to see more Filipinos allowed to immigrate. But I am a citizen here. The bucket is getting empty. If we cannot balance our budget, if we cannot put things in order in this country, how can we always help the rest of the world?"

✶

The last time I drove across America was exactly thirty years earlier. My law-school roommate, Paul Tagliabue, and I had been recruited by a Los Angeles law firm to spend the summer as clerks. The firm sent us two round-trip first-class airplane tickets, which we promptly cashed in, using the proceeds to rent a red convertible. We made most of the same stops in 1964 that I made on this trip in 1994 including my grandfather's farm in Cassville and Mount Rushmore.

When Paul and I made that drive, it was a good deal harder for one large segment of America—African Americans—to say with enthusiasm, "We are all Americans." This was the time of sit-ins at drugstore counters and restaurants. And for good reason. The college I had attended, Vanderbilt, had been officially segregated by race in its undergraduate classes until 1962. I realized that at many of the restaurants where Paul and I ate, the motels where we slept, black Americans might not have been welcome.

Paul, who is now the commissioner of the National

Football League, grew up in Jersey City. His parents came to this country from northern Italy. His father was a contractor in Union City. His mother was a seamstress, who became so concerned about the frayed collars on my shirts that she turned them one night while I slept at the Tagliabue house. To prepare him for playground basketball—and perhaps to prepare him for life—Paul's father insisted that he slam his elbows against the concrete walls in the basement. This served Paul well as captain of Georgetown University's basketball team. I imagine it also serves him well today in owners' meetings.

About three years ago Paul was to be an honoree at the Italian-American dinner in Washington, D.C. He invited me to go. I was not, to tell you the truth, looking forward to one more long Washington dinner. But looking back, I wouldn't have missed it for the world. There was a boisterous room filled with men and women bursting with pride in their Italian heritage. There were cheers for Scalia, the justice. For Stallone, the actor. For Tagliabue, the commissioner. For Pelosi, the congresswoman. They were all there.

But what struck me most about the evening was not just the pride in their Italian heritage. It was their pride in America. This pride was spontaneous and unembarrassed. You felt it in the singing of the national anthem, in the recitation of the Pledge of Allegiance, and in all the speeches. They all knew where they had come from. More important, they all knew where they were now and why they were here. This was a celebration of the promise of American life. No one in the room doubted that this country had an unlimited future, and that every single person in the room and their sons and their daughters and their grandchildren could have a piece of that future if they would only work.

I wished that every American could have gone with me to that Italian-American dinner. It would make it much easier for everyone to say those four magic words: We Are All Americans. It reminded me of Fred Montgomery's blessing before the Fourth of July fried-fish supper in Henning.

LAMAR ALEXANDER WITH RUTH ZIOLKOWSKI
PHOTOGRAPH BY EARL WARREN

CHAPTER 11

Keeping the Dream Alive

CUSTER, South Dakota

Leaving Sioux City it had turned cold. The rain had blown through and there was every color of green along Interstate 29—soybean green, cornstalk green, mesquite green, the green of the sage, and of the grass and of the blowing reeds. There was a tinge of brown to herald the winter. There were splotches of yellow black-eyed Susans where the fields had not been cut.

For 176 miles from Rankin City, we had almost no company except the old state highway running alongside. Recently rolled round bales of hay were the only signs of life.

Finally, we reached the Black Hills. These mountains are much like the Great Smokies, where I grew up, but without the hardwoods. Mainly there are spruce and pine growing out of dry earth, without so much rain and without the gnats that come with the rain in the Smokies. Some of these Black Hills are great granite bluffs. One of the bluffs is Mount Rushmore.

It had been thirty years since I had seen Mount Rushmore. This is a monument on a truly outrageous scale, conceived in 1923 when America was cocky and confident and dreaming and talking big. From the first dynamite blast in 1927 until 1941, there were workers with jackhammers hanging over the sides of these mountains, blowing chunks of rock away. It is the conspicuous symbol of this country's bold spirit and sweeping aspirations.

Driving along you first see the face of Washington, sixty feet from chin to hairline, imagining—I was thinking—that there could be a country such as ours. Then Jefferson, facing back toward you, imagining what that country could be. Then Lincoln, imagining that it was worth saving. And when you have driven around the curve, there is Teddy Roosevelt, imagining that we could do just about anything.

*

South Dakota Governor Bill Janklow had told me the night before: "If you go to Mount Rushmore, you have to see Crazy Horse." And so off we went that morning, headed toward Custer, taking the governor's advice. Five miles north of Custer we turned left on the Avenue of the Chiefs, and this sign appeared: NOT A STATE OR

166

FEDERAL PROJECT. A NON-PROFIT CORPORATION FOR THE BENEFIT OF THE INDIAN PEOPLE OF AMERICA. As our eyes climbed a solid wall of granite more than a mile away, an unfinished face began to emerge near the top of Thunderhead Mountain. To be honest, we had to imagine a face. Although the sculptor, Korczak Ziolkowski, began carving the mountain in 1948, it still takes a pretty good imagination to see what he and his family and associates have been working on for nearly half a century.

This is the face of the legendary Indian chief Crazy Horse, one of the strategists of the Battle of Little Big Horn. When the task is finished, this monument will be ten times larger than the one on Rushmore. It will be 563 feet high and 641 feet wide.

*

Time seemed to have no meaning for Korczak, which is what everyone has always called the sculptor. He had traveled from Connecticut to South Dakota in 1939 to assist Gutzon Borglum in carving the faces of Washington, Jefferson, Lincoln, and Roosevelt. He then volunteered for World War II and returned to Connecticut. In 1939 he received a letter from Henry Standing Bear, then a chief of the Sioux, inviting him to return to South Dakota and carve a fifth face in the Black Hills. "My fellow chiefs and I would like the white man to know that the red man has great heroes, too," wrote Standing Bear.

Korczak immediately accepted Standing Bear's invitation and came to the Black Hills to dedicate the rest of his life to carving a monumental face of the chief who never surrendered, never signed a treaty, and refused to live on a reservation. Crazy Horse was stabbed in the back by a white soldier while under a flag of truce. He died just after midnight on September 6, 1877, thirty-one years to the day before Korczak was born.

Korczak's first dynamite blast on Thunderhead Mountain was June 3, 1948. "I wanted to tell the story of the North American Indian," he said shortly before his death in 1982. Since then, his wife, Ruth, and seven of their ten children have continued to carve the mountain.

"The face will be finished by the year 2000," Ruth Ziolkowski assured us. She had met us just outside the sixty-one-room house/museum that she and Korczak had built for their children and their visitors. We parked the Explorer and went inside to watch a promotional film about Korczak and his project.

*

He was born in Boston, the son of Polish immigrants. Orphaned at three, he grew up in a series of foster homes, without training in the art of sculpting. He was totally self-taught. He might have settled for a life of ease and acclaim after he won first prize at the New York World's Fair in 1939 for his bust of Jan Paderewski, the Polish pianist.

When the war started, he was hired by Pratt and

Whitney Aircraft to work in their experimental hangar. At thirty-four, too old to be drafted, he volunteered. His request for duty as a paratrooper was rejected, and he wound up with an antiaircraft battery and spent three years in France and Germany. He took part in the invasion of Normandy and landed on Omaha Beach.

Even then, he was irrepressible. His unit was camped outside Rouen, on the road to Paris, and he heard that General George Patton, one of his heroes, was in the area. He wanted to go AWOL and meet Patton, but he couldn't convince his crew to join him. Instead, he found a tree stump and carved it into a six-foot statue of Charles de Gaulle. The last anyone heard, the tree stump is on display in a museum in Paris. How it got there, no one is quite certain.

When he returned to South Dakota to begin work on Crazy Horse, he spent $6,000 of his life savings to buy 650 acres of land and mining rights to Thunderhead. He had $174 left to his name the day he set off the first charge of dynamite. Five of the survivors of the battle at Little Big Horn attended the dedication ceremonies.

The Indians were thrilled to see this awesome task undertaken, the white townspeople and the rest of America less so. Donations the first year averaged just five cents per visitor. Korczak had to impose a modest admission charge. To raise more funds, he built a dairy farm and a lumber mill.

Korczak was nearly forty when he started drilling away the rock. Where he made his camp, there was nothing, no roads, no water or electricity. High on the mountain, he worked alone for years. He lived in a tent for seven months. Each day he would carry a drill and green lumber up a 741-step staircase that he himself had constructed. The drill was driven by a small bullet compressor which stayed at the bottom of the mountain.

"The compressor would stop several times a day," Ruth told us, forcing him to run back down those 741 steps and then back up again. "People used to wonder why in his pictures he is always smiling." Mountain goats kept him company, and are still there today despite the decades of blasting.

Ruth was a young student from Connecticut when she arrived with a group of volunteers in 1949 to assist Korczak. They were married the next year and raised five sons and five daughters. "One of them he delivered himself," Ruth said.

When he died at seventy-four, he left Ruth and the children three notebooks filled with instructions on how to continue the work. His last words were: "Crazy Horse must be finished. You must work on the mountain; but go slowly, so you do it right."

Ruth is now five years younger than her husband was when he died. She runs the center, the project, and the family, and her children and grandchildren work alongside her, some on the mountain, some on the ground.

Ruth was going to drive the car I was in, and she made a point of saying, "I know you're going to try to be polite and hold the door, but you get in first. That way you can see what's going on."

As we wound our way up the road, Ruth gave me a short narrative of life in the shadow of Crazy Horse: "We cut our own timber, build our own roads, supply our own water. It's like running a small city. Up the top of this hill, we've dug a hole which can take a 150,000-gallon water tank and it's 160 feet higher than the house. We have all the pressure we need for water and to fight fires. We have our own security, our own sewer system. We're independent. Can't work much in the winter, but we've been snowed in only twice, all the years I've been here, which is not a bad record.

"When Korczak went on trips, he always took one or two of the kids with him. This is a great place to raise a family, but they needed to know there's something on the other side of the mountain."

When I asked how she, and her husband before her, could devote their lives to a project they would not see finished, she said cheerfully: "Well, you divide it into stages. We hope the face is finished by 1998, which would be our fiftieth anniversary. If not, by the year 2000. You look at it in little steps. Each step is progress. I think I'm the luckiest person in the world. I love what I do. It's never the same twice. And it's a challenge and an inspiration to a lot of people." She nodded as we passed a young man standing near the road and said, "That's Mark."

"Mark?"

"One of our sons. He is more like his dad than any

171

of the others. Mark is the one who clears the timber, builds the roads, and all that. Monique is a sculptor. Casimir oversees the blasting and the carving. He could be a sculptor if he wanted. Marinka is a painter. I can't draw a straight line with a ruler. We have two who write poetry. Dawn organizes the tours and Anne manages the museum. There are four who raise beautiful children and do different things. The fact that seven of them are still involved in the project is a tribute to their father. He was such a perfectionist."

The car stopped and we got out and walked around. Ruth sent someone ahead to get the attention of the construction workers and let them know we were visitors. It was hard to believe that we were standing on the arm of Crazy Horse.

"His arm?" I repeated.

She nodded. "About four thousand men could stand on this arm. It's ninety feet from his chin to his hairline. If you divide your face into thirds, his nose is about thirty feet long. They drill and blast, or use feather drills and wedges to spread the rock out. Then to polish it they use the torch, which is the noise you heard as we were driving up. It heats to 3400 degrees and just kind of scalds the rock."

The arm is the length of a football field, but measured in tons and decades. The numbers are so staggering I am not sure that they convey any meaningful perspective: The single eagle feather in Crazy Horse's hair is forty-four feet high, a free-standing pillar, man-made from huge blast fragments. The head of the horse is twenty-two stories high; a five-story house would fit inside the flaring nostril.

For an instant, I felt like a pimple on a presidential nose. The faces on Mount Rushmore are sixty feet high. All four would fit inside the head of Crazy Horse.

I said, "When your husband started this in 1948, you had to use a lot of imagination."

"You had to imagine it all," she said. "Now it's so nice. People can drive up and say, 'Well, I can see his [Crazy Horse's] nose. And in the morning when the light is right, you can see his eye from down here. And you have the outline of his face. Korczak made the model of Crazy Horse on his horse to fit the shape of the mountain, because the rock you leave here doesn't cost any money. What you have to blast off is expensive."

No one is yet certain what the final cost will be, but the investment to date has passed the $10 million figure. "And we've raised every penny of it from contributions and people coming here," emphasized Ruth. "Never a cent from the state or federal governments."

This work in progress now attracts over a million and a quarter tourists a year. Once a year, in June, they are allowed to climb the mountain. More than eight thousand made the attempt in 1994.

There are about fifty names on the waiting list of volunteers who want to work on the project. "Everybody thinks they would love to work here," says Ruth. "A lot of them would like to come and work for a week or two just to say they did it. That's the kind you can't afford. It takes a summer to train someone."

She says the sheer magnitude of the job attracts the finest engineers and demolition people in the country. A veteran of the army's Special Services Branch, who once taught at the FBI Academy, is in charge of explosives.

They drill holes that are up to seventy-two feet deep. It takes three days to drill, lay out the patterns, set off the blast, and clear the debris from the ledge.

"I wonder where all the people with these big ideas are today?" I said, shading my eyes as I looked up the nose of Crazy Horse.

"Oh, they're around," said Ruth, "you just have to find 'em. Of course, I'll grant you there are not many of them carving a mountain."

"But what an outrageous and magnificent idea," I said. "Imagine thinking of something this huge and actually doing it."

"A little Indian who didn't have enough to eat was the one who had the dream in the first place," she said.

She was referring, of course, to Henry Standing Bear. After we had driven back down the mountain, Ruth led us through the Indian museum attached to her house. She showed me a wooden plaque that reproduced an enlargement of the original letter he had sent to Korczak, which said, in part:

According to newspaper notice, I note you have won honors at the New York World's Fair in sculpture work. A number of my fellow chiefs and I are interested in finding some sculptor who can carve the head of an Indian chief who was killed many years ago. The proposition is mine to be pushed by these certain chiefs and myself under my direction. Would you care to correspond with me on this project?

There is a great deal to be explained, of course. Perhaps you can help me in some way. This to be entirely an Indian project. Please write at your earliest convenience. As a matter of long standing in my mind, which must be brought before the public soon, the main thing now is to know if someone can do the work. . . .

Very truly,
Henry Standing Bear

The letter was dated November 7, 1939. A second letter contained his plaintive words: "My fellow chiefs and I would like the white man to know the red man has great heroes, too."

Korczak responded: "The treatment of the American Indian is the blackest mark on our nation's history. If by carving Crazy Horse, I can give back to the Indians some of their pride, my life will have been worthwhile."

In 1989, eight electrical companies wired the mountain with lights, and Philips Lighting keeps them stocked with bulbs. "We send them the burned-out ones," says Ruth, "and they replace them." The late Malcolm Forbes, publisher, sportsman, and philanthropist, threw the switch to turn on the lights for the first time.

"He was one of the most delightful gentlemen I've ever met," said Ruth. "He was out here with his hot air balloon and his motorcycle. Someone was trying to decide what to give someone like Malcolm Forbes for his birthday. Well, we came up with it. He turned on the lights and it made for a bright evening."

In the winter, when the operation pretty much shuts down, the professionals on the crew take other jobs. "You can't tell the crew to go home in November and just come back in May. They have families that have to eat, too. So if we have to, we manufacture a job."

Three members of the crew went down to Georgia three years ago to clean up Stone Mountain, in preparation for the 1996 Olympics in Atlanta.

"If he were starting over today, in 1994," I asked Ruth, "could Korczak begin to carve his monument of Crazy Horse?"

She did not hesitate. "No, he couldn't," said Ruth. "The government, OSHA, all those things would have gotten in the way. All of the studies that you would have to do to find out whether it was environmentally sound to carve a mountain. No, I don't think you would have much of a chance. Oh, if his mind was set, he would have done it, but it would have been a heck of a lot harder. Of course, we've been at it close to fifty years, so I don't know how much harder it could get.

"But Korczak was a firm believer that you can do anything in the world you want to do. Doesn't make

176

any difference what it is. You get up in the morning
and you go to work. You can't quit. You have to stick
with it. You have to be willing to work. And there is
nothing you can't do."

I asked her my question: "Looking ahead twenty
years, do you believe these children and your grandchildren will have more opportunity growing up in this
country than you and Korczak did?"

"I would like to think this country is going to get
straightened out," she said. "And I don't necessarily
think it is a Republican or a Democratic problem. It is
a people problem. Somehow we have got to get the
economy under control. I mean, I look at this project
and health insurance just with our little group of people. You look at what you spend that you never see,
and I don't know how it can continue the way it's going.
I really don't. I was shocked the other day. We have one
person on our payroll who is in the logging business.
The insurance on that alone, for workmen's compensation, is fifty-one percent of his wages. Now that is
outrageous! I think we need to get back to good old-
fashioned common sense.

"And you can't take care of everybody. There are people who need help. No question about it. I'd be the first
one to say fine, we need to help them. But there are so
many things that need to be done in this country, if you
want a handout and you're capable of work, then you
ought to work. But I have faith that, somehow or other,
it's going to get turned around."

Korczak believed that every time the government in

177

Washington makes a decision for you, it takes away your freedom to make that decision for yourself. That is why he pursued his magnificent dream without government help. He preferred to trudge up and down 741 steps several times a day carrying a drill and green lumber than run the risk that someone in Washington would interfere with his freedom to complete his project as he saw fit.

"Korczak was the ultimate believer in the free-enterprise system," Ruth said. "Twice he was offered ten million dollars in federal money to finish the project but he turned it down. He thought the government would never finish the project. At least he was sure that it would have some different ideas about it. He wanted to build the face his way, and then he imagined a huge North American Indian Center, with a university and a medical complex.

"He once told them, 'I have copies of three hundred and sixty-five treaties made with the Indians. Am I to believe you would keep this one?' When he was working on Rushmore, Borglum used to spend a lot of time in Washington," she recalled, "wining and dining officials. Korczak found that repulsive."

"When legends die," Korczak wrote before his death, quoting a French philosopher, "dreams end. When dreams end, there is no greatness." Korczak was determined that no one in Washington, D.C., would step on that dream.

✳

As we drove away from Thunderhead Mountain I thought of my grandfather Rankin. So far as I know, he never thought of carving a mountain, but some of his dreams—and his actions—were nearly as outrageous. He was the one who ran away from his home in the Tennessee mountains when he was eleven, made his way to Texas, became a railroad engineer, and finally made his way back to Tennessee in time to instruct all of us growing up: "Aim for the top. There's more room there."

That is why we grew up thinking any of us could be a railroad engineer, or a school principal like my dad, or the Kiwanis Club president, or the president of the United States. I am sure if someone had suggested carving a face on the side of a granite mountain in South Dakota, we would have seen no reason why that would not have been possible, too. I believe my grandfather and Korczak would have understood each other. I believe that each had about the same view of what the possibilities are in America and what it takes to realize those possibilities.

I wish today that I could ask both men, Korczak and my grandfather, whether they believe the future generations will have more opportunity growing up in this country than they had.

I am confident their answer would be yes, absolutely yes, with one proviso—and that is, that we stop trying to reinvent America in Washington, D.C., and start remembering what made this such a remarkable country in the first place. I can't imagine a better way to re-

179

member this than to drive through the Black Hills of South Dakota. First to Rushmore, where the four presidential faces in granite are still the best reminder of our boldness and sweeping aspirations and of the kind of leadership it takes to realize those aspirations. Then to Thunderhead Mountain, where the face of Crazy Horse is emerging just in time to remind us that we will get to the top in the next century the same way we always have: with magnificent dreams and the freedom and determination to keep those dreams alive.

Epilogue

It has been exactly one year since I began my drive across America. My life has changed considerably because I am now a candidate for president of the United States. To give you just one example of that change: Not long ago, after a long day of campaigning, I arrived in Marietta, Georgia, well after midnight. The local committee insisted that I stay in a bed and breakfast, and the lady who owned it insisted that I wake up in time to try her "special muffins." So early the next morning I stumbled downstairs. There was the lady, the kitchen table, the "special muffins," a pitcher of orange juice, the coffee, and the coffee cup. I proceeded to do something I had never done before nor am ever likely to do again—I picked up the orange juice and poured it into the coffee cup. The lady looked at me a long time and finally said, "I sure hope you're not running for anything big!"

∗

The next president will be the first president of the next century. His job is to help our country recapture its confidence. To do that, he must remind us that it is not necessary to reinvent America in Washington, D.C., but to remember what made this such a great country in the first place. Those things are: a growing economy that creates jobs, more freedom from Washington to plan our own lives, and a citizenship that understands the importance of personal responsibility.

These are the three areas upon which I would focus my attention as president:

1. Jobs and Growth. I would start, just as I did as governor, with jobs. That is the first concern in the everyday lives of most Americans. Father Jerry Hill in Dallas and I agree: The world changed about 1980. He saw it from the homeless shelter; I saw it from the governor's mansion. The telecommunications age and world competition turned the American workplace upside down. Companies downsized, jobs skills changed, and 10 percent of Americans began losing their jobs every year. In most families, every parent went to work outside the home. Although people were working harder, the standard of living for many families seemed to drop. College graduates found the job market a real jungle. In 1992 I remember telling some of President Bush's economic advisers, "If the president goes out and says that the economy is getting better he will be technically correct, but everyone will think he doesn't know what is going on." The economy may have been better, but the voters weren't feeling better. A great many Americans driving to work then and today sometimes wonder if they will have a job when they get there.

I know growth is the answer because I have seen it work. When I was governor, my focus from the first day to the last was on raising family incomes. That meant recruiting the Nissan and Saturn auto plants. But, most important, it meant creating an environment in which new jobs could grow. We changed usury limits and banking laws, built hundreds of miles of interstate highways with our own money, reduced debt, reduced the number of state employees, earned a AAA bond rating, and kept our taxes fifth lowest in the country.

We learned quickly that better schools mean better jobs. That meant computers in the classrooms, new standards and tests, summer programs for gifted students, high admission standards at colleges, chairs of excellence at the universities. When Saturn came and someone asked its president, "Why Tennessee?," he said, "Because they pay teachers more for teaching well and that's the kind of environment in which we want to try to build cars that compete with the best Japanese and German cars." Today, my successor—a Democrat—will proudly tell you that for the last ten years, family incomes in our state have grown more rapidly than in any other. We've gone from never having made a car to being the third-largest producer of automobiles. In 1986, *National Geographic's* cover story proclaimed RISING SHINING TENNESSEE. On my drive I stopped in Cambridge, Massachusetts, to talk with Dr. David Birch, who studies job growth and loss and who annually compiles a list of "entrepreneurial hot spots." He said Tennessee has risen from "off the charts at the bottom" in the early 1980s to seventh among hot spots for growing companies. Dr. Birch, and most others who have watched our state, believe our policies in the 1980s of encouraging growth and focusing on education made the difference.

After I left the governor's office in 1987, I helped start a private company from scratch. Five of us (including Bob Keeshan, "Captain Kangaroo") came up with an idea, put a little money in, and recruited capital and managers and customers. In less than a decade our little company—which helps large companies provide child care for their employees—has created 1,200 jobs. For the last three years it has been on *Inc.* magazine's list of fast-growing small companies. This is the way that almost every single one of the new jobs in America is created today: by rapidly growing small companies.

As president, my objective would be to create an environment in which such growing companies can generate the largest number of good new jobs. That means a flatter, simpler, fairer federal income tax to stimulate the savings and investment that help create jobs. It means cutting the capital gains tax in half. (Republicans are much too timid about this. A capital gains tax cut would create a Niagara Falls of new jobs.) It means speeding up regulatory decision making and, in some cases, just wiping the regulatory slate clean and starting over. Sometimes I believe regulations take as much money out of our pockets as taxes do.

Of course I would balance the budget—which would help keep interest rates low and reduce the growth of government. As governor, I balanced the budget eight years in a row. It is utterly foolish for the federal government to continue to spend $600 million more per day than it brings in. Members of Congress don't deserve an award for balancing the budget any more than Boy Scouts deserve a badge for telling the truth. It's their job.

Nothing is more important to creating growth and jobs than a first-class system of education to which everyone has reasonable access. The good news for our country is we already have almost all the best colleges and universities. And while it is never easy to pay for college, half our college students have federal grants and loans, and many of our educational programs—such as community colleges—have tuitions of a few hundred dollars per quarter. This is one reason why we are still the world grand champion in science and technology.

The bad news is that our system of elementary and secondary schools needs a radical overhaul. Almost everybody knows this but, for the amount of energy expended, not much is getting done to make things better. That is why I would end Washington's involvement in elementary and secondary education, and put all the decisions and money back in the hands of parents, teachers, and communities. As president, I would become the nation's chief advocate for radical change in education: Give parents the money we spend on schools and let them choose the school that best fits their child; pay teachers more for teaching well; open schools all day every day, and let parents choose among—and pay for—the extra educational hours; welcome the private sector to help create even better schools. None of this should be federal law; all of it should be the president's education agenda.

2. Washington, D.C. The need to send education dollars and decision making home is a reminder of the second big problem we face: Washington, D.C. Washington spends too much, meddles too much, and spends too much time telling us we are too stupid to make decisions for ourselves. On almost every stop along my drive I heard this same story. Father Hill in Dallas will not take a federal grant anymore because he doesn't want to spend all day Friday filling out forms to justify what he did Monday through Thursday. The district attorney in East Baton Rouge is wary of federal crime bills because of the restrictions they bring. The small college president in Iowa is sitting there exasperated, facing a stack of new regulations from Washington that had just arrived in the mail in a shrink-wrapped package.

We should not only move all of elementary and secondary education out of Washington, D.C., but most law enforcement as well. We should end welfare in Washington, not just fix it there one more time. The $25 billion Washington spends on job training would be better spent by turning the money into vouchers for people losing or changing jobs and letting them take the money to an employer and say: "Here. Train me." The best training for work is work. I would like to see a six-month citizen Congress.

I believe any Congress, including a Republican Congress, would be a better Congress if it spent more time at home and less time in Washington. A citizen Congress and term limits would permanently change the culture of Washington, D.C. (Imagine Ellis Cormier, "The Boudin King," in the U.S. House of Representatives!)

Unfortunately, Potomac fever can infect Republicans, too. Some Washington Republicans want to tell states how to run their welfare programs. They also say, "If you want Washington money for prisons, let Washington set state criminal sentences." I think these things are none of Washington's business. That's simply substituting Republican orders from Washington for Democratic orders. We are not too stupid in our own communities to make those decisions for ourselves. The greatest danger we have as a party now that we have captured Washington is that Washington might capture us.

3. Personal Responsibility. The third problem we face is a lack of personal responsibility. On my drive, I heard a great deal about the arrogance of Washington, D.C. But I heard even more about the breakdown of the family. People may not want their politicians lecturing them about this, but everyone knows it is true. Walk outside your house and ask ten people what they believe is the greatest problem facing our country today. I believe most of them will tell you it is the breakdown of the family. When the family, neighborhood, churches, and school are broken, the most essential suppliers of our country's spirit and confidence are broken.

Here again, we know what to do. Stop the federal government from undermining responsibility. Misty and Aaron in Cassville, Missouri, thinking about having their first child, will tell you it destroys incentive when their friends on welfare who are sitting at home are better off than *they* are, working fifty-six hours a week. Father Hill is outraged that the government in Washington is spending $446 per month on Social Security disability benefits for drug addicts who then want to find their way into his shelter. "How can I help them," he says, "when they have that kind of support for their dependency?" Reuben Greenberg, the Charleston police chief, had to fight with Washington for two years to get permission to kick mothers on welfare who sell crack out of his housing projects so mothers who follow the law can live safely with their children. Reverend Henry Delaney, the "five hundred pounds of prophecy," wonders why someone doesn't ask him what to do about the welfare system rather than overhaul it one more time in Washington. He thinks he knows how to help people get back up on their feet in Savannah.

Washington is one place to begin, but the other place to start is you and me. When I stopped in Henning on that first night of my drive, they were talking about their first drive-by shooting. No one thought a federal crime bill would help. No one suggested calling the governor. They were talking about a curfew for their own children, or a community code of parental responsibility, or a city ordinance that made every parent responsible if their child damaged someone else's property.

My pet peeve is that almost every American school still operates from about 8:00 A.M. to 3:00 P.M. In the working world, that fits almost no family's schedule. Most of us know instinctively what chief Reuben Greenberg has proved once again: If kids are busy, they get into less trouble, have less opportunity to get pregnant, to try drugs, to shoot each other. So why aren't the schools open all day every day? Especially when communities like Murfreesboro, Tennessee, have proved it can be done without one extra penny of cost to the taxpayer. (Parents pay and no poor family is turned away.) We aren't doing what we know to do.

As I write this, there have been nearly two weeks of news about trash on television and excessive violence and sexual innuendo in movies. Of course this is true. Of course it harms children. Of course it damages our culture. But a speech about Hollywood values is only half a speech. The other half is even more important. We don't have to go to the movies. We can turn off the television. If our child isn't learning, we can read to him. If the child isn't home at night, we can find out where she is. Thirty percent of the babies born in the largest women's hospital in Michigan are exposed to cocaine because their mothers have been using crack. I don't think this is a Washington, D.C., problem. This is our problem. If all we do is blame someone else for these things, we will never get our country back on track.

*

Of course, one of the president's main responsibilities is always as commander in chief and the spokesman for America's responsibilities in world affairs. Especially in these times, there can be no such thing as a "domestic president" or a "foreign policy president"; things at home and overseas are much too interrelated for that. But a president capable of making good executive decisions would greatly improve the discharge of our responsibilities in the world.

First, the president should fire the pollsters and assemble a first-rate team of experts in foreign policy and national security affairs. The president is not expected to be an expert in these matters, but he is expected to know who is—and with their advice, formulate a set of goals and strategies and stick to them. He must strengthen relationships with our old allies and build new relationships, especially with Russia and China. Stop the free fall in defense spending—we are the world's only superpower. And don't give an inch to the rogue nations: North Korea, Iran, and Iraq.

We are the only superpower, but we are not the world's policeman. We should be keeping peace only when there is peace to keep. Our operating rule should be this: We should not become involved in someone else's civil war on the other side of the world unless we are prepared to pick a side and win the battle.

We know what to do.

*

Those faces on Mount Rushmore that Korczak Ziolkowski helped to carve remind us that when our fathers and mothers "brought forth on this continent a new nation," they began a journey to freedom, freedom from governmental tyranny and oppression, freedom for personal responsibility. One freedom simply cannot exist without the other. This great journey, this incred-

191

ible experiment we call America, has never stopped. All of us have all participated in this journey, not knowing exactly where it was heading, always moving forward with confidence and courage, and always being certain of one thing: that America has an unlimited future and that every single one of us can have a part of that future. That is the promise of American life.

Somehow, somewhere, we've gotten off track. Lost our way. Too many are losing that courage, that confidence, and much of that hope. I believe there is no excuse for this. I believe there has never been a period of greater opportunity. The faces of those I met on my drive remind me that we know what to do. We may not have all the answers, but we have enough to get started, and the will and the courage to find the rest.

I do not think of the people I met in small towns and big cities as winners of special merit badges or as exceptions to the rule. They exemplify the American way of life, working every day as reminders of how we recover and strengthen that irrational belief in our unlimited future.

Recapturing the promise of American life is a constant endeavor that mostly must take place at home, in churches and synagogues, in the neighborhood. It relies on the unwavering determination of each of us to do the best we can for our own families, our own communities, and ourselves.

That is why the next president—the first president of the next century—must do much more than turn Washington off. The next president must find a way to turn all of America on—not only get Washington off our backs, but get us back into our families, neighborhoods, churches, and schools. We have settled for Washington's best long enough. It has come close to doing us in. Washington has stolen our confidence from us. What we need is America's best. That's our people. Every one of us.

The most important faces of the next century are not the faces on Mount Rushmore—or even the face of the next president—but the faces of Father Hill and Reuben Greenberg, of Reverend Delaney and Dan Biederman, of Henry Ronquillo and Larry Joyce, of Ruth Ziolkowski and her children, and of countless more of our fellow citizens whose lives attest to their belief that tomorrow can be made better than today for every participant in the American experiment.

—LAMAR ALEXANDER
Nashville
July 4, 1995

Acknowledgments

There are literally hundreds of people to whom I owe thanks for being a part of my drive across America—and this book. Many of them made it possible. Lots of them made it colorful. Others simply made it enjoyable. All helped reinforce my sense that we do, in fact, know what to do. Here I can thank some of these people by name, but by no means will these few paragraphs exhaust the list of men and women who have my deep appreciation.

I am especially grateful to the dozens of people all across America who put me up for the night or spent long hours talking. By their generosity, not only did I get much-needed rest and wonderful home-cooked meals; I also learned from every one of them. They include Fred and Ernestine Montgomery of Henning, Tennessee; my great-aunt Sula, cousin Larry Mac Edens, and his wife, Lonna, in Cassville, Missouri; Father Jerry Hill, in Dallas, Texas; The Boudin King, Ellis Cormier, and his wife, June, of Jennings, Louisiana; Sharon and Charlie Ross of Jackson, Mississippi; Betty and Ted Nickinson in Pensacola, Florida; Savannah, Georgia's Reverend Henry O. and Ethel Delaney; Laura and Chris Lindsey, of Wilmington, Delaware; Evelyn and Rollie Balanza, of Fair Lawn, New Jersey; the Griffin Family of Bedford, New Hampshire; Wisconsin Governor Tommy Thompson; Ruth and Jerry Welter of Monticello, Iowa; former Tennesseans John and Virginia Runne, who have transplanted themselves to Evergreen, Colorado; Tom Fuentes of Costa Mesa, California; and Theodore Roosevelt High School principal Henry Ronquillo and his wife, Margaret, of Los Angeles, California.

Thanks also to: Slick Lawson; William Nelson; Angie Hadley; Misty and Aaron Gates; Bill, Bob, and Jackson Brumley; Emory Melton; Ross Swimmer; Jan Langbein; Doug Moreau; Elmer Litchfield; Bishop Knox; Jerry Hatcher; Reuben Greenberg; Ruth and Daniel J. Boorstin; Peggy Noonan; Dan Biederman; Tom Kean; David Birch; Richard M. Flynn; Ray Wieczorek; Andrea and Hugh Lee; Charles Everett; Steve Morris; Father James Grandillo; Julie Sullens and the staff of Detroit's Hutzel Hospital; J.B. (Bronce) Henderson; Larry Joyce; Dr. George Sweeting and the Moody Bible College; Robb

Rauh, Alma Walton, and Milwaukee's Urban Day School; Joe Ertl; Mary Andringa; Lew and Steve Throssel; Jean and Gene Wiese; Gary Griffis; Ruth Ziolkowski; Ben Houston; Phil Burgess; Andy Bane; the Scott McInness Family; Sister Jennie Lechtenberg; and eight UCLA students who got up early on a Saturday morning to come talk with me.

During my trip I also took time to meet with some of the hosts of the Republican Neighborhood Meeting, the satellite television program I started in 1993. Many of the topics I discussed on the monthly broadcast were inspired by the conversations I had and the places I visited while driving across the country

Great thanks are also due to the dozens of people who helped organize the drive—or who helped hold down the home and office forts during the two months I was on the road. I am very grateful to those who joined me on all or part of that road. The group included Lewis Lavine, our chief planner and chief navigator much of the time; John Danielson, an unflappable and reliable friend; my elder son, Drew, who came along for a few thousand miles; his friend Rob Gluck, who did us the favor of driving up only one mountain pass with the emergency brake on; Ohio native Karin Markey, who steered us through the Rust Belt; photographer Earl Warren, who took most of the photographs that are part of this book and who often took the wheel when I needed time to do some writing; and Scott Hamil-

197

ton, whose notes, comments, tape-recording skills, and pondering contributed to this book.

This book would not have been possible without Mickey Herskowitz. I gathered the stories on the drive. Mickey helped select and organize the stories that we chose to tell. We wrote the book together. What I like best about Mickey is that he has a sportswriter's knack for seeing and telling a wonderful story and writing in plain, non–Washington, D.C., prose. William Morrow and Company and editor Will Schwalbe understood from the beginning the different kind of book I wanted to write. My agent, Sherry Arden, literally made it all possible. Daniel Casse reviewed the entire manuscript and offered thoughtful criticism. Chester E. Finn, Jr., helped find the right ways to tell the stories and the lessons from them. Many thanks to each of them.

For almost two years, I have been a Senior Fellow and chairman of the project on "The New Promise of American Life" at Hudson Institute in Indianapolis, Indiana. That project—and its support of a portion of my drive—have contributed greatly to my thinking and to this book. I am grateful to Hudson and its president, Leslie Lenkowsky.

In the dedication of this book I try to express how much I am grateful for the love and support and patience from our family members—especially to Honey—for these unusual adventures I regularly get myself, and them, into.

I should also say a word of thanks to the University of Tennessee Volunteers, who almost gave us a great come-from-behind victory in a football game against UCLA in the Rose Bowl that marked the end of my two-month drive.

Finally, let me acknowledge Wendy Steuck, who succeeded when everyone else had failed to free my colleague John Danielson, who had locked himself in the bathroom of the S&A Convenience gas station in Canton, South Dakota. She knew what to do.

About the Author

Lamar Alexander has been governor, university president, and U.S. education secretary. He and his wife, Honey, helped found a company, Corporate Child Care, which today has twelve hundred employees.

In 1978 he walked one thousand miles across Tennessee to become its governor. At the request of the U.S. attorney, he was sworn into office three days early to prevent the incumbent governor from granting clemency to prisoners the FBI believed had paid cash for their release.

During his two terms as governor, Tennessee increased the number of jobs at twice the national average, went from last to third in the production of new automobiles, from forty-third to thirty-sixth in average personal income, and enacted the nation's only state program to pay teachers more for teaching well. When he left office, the state had fewer government employees, a smaller debt, and the nation's fifth lowest tax rate.

He and his family then moved to Australia to live for a while and he wrote his third book, *Six Months Off*, about that experience. In 1988 he became president of the University of Tennessee. And in 1991 the U.S. Senate unanimously confirmed him as President Bush's education secretary.

He is a country and classical pianist who has played at the Grand Ole Opry and the Billy Graham Crusade. He chaired the nation's governors, served as co-director of Empower America, and founded the Republican Neighborhood Meeting. The Education Commission of the States and the National Collegiate Athletic Association have given him their highest awards. He lives in Nashville. The Alexanders have four children: Andrew, twenty-five; Leslee, twenty-three; Kathryn, twenty-one; and William, sixteen.